Chicago Hopeless

BY
Shirley J. Thompson

PublishAmerica
Baltimore

© 2005 by Shirley J. Thompson.
All rights reserved. No part of this book may be reproduced, stored in a retrieval system or transmitted in any form or by any means without the prior written permission of the publishers, except by a reviewer who may quote brief passages in a review to be printed in a newspaper, magazine or journal.

First printing

This is a true story. However, the names of all medical personnel and locations have been changed in order to protect thier pirvacy.

ISBN: 1-4137-8771-1
PUBLISHED BY PUBLISHAMERICA, LLLP
www.publishamerica.com
Baltimore

Printed in the United States of America

DEDICATION

To the memory of my sister, Betty, who passed away in December 2002. Your courage and the ability to laugh and make fun of what life tossed in your direction will always be an inspiration to me. You continued to hound me to get this book published. I'm sorry you won't be able to see the book in print, but I feel I had your help in getting this far.

To my sister, Lois, who staunchly supported us during our ordeal, who traveled with us, took care of us, and was the rock that we needed to anchor us to reality.

To my family, which continues to support me and encourage my writing.

To my co-workers, who read each chapter as it was completed and begged for more.

To my nephew, Jeff, who was his mother's main caregiver during her many recoveries from surgery. It is not easy being a caregiver. It is a thankless job with many demands constantly taking precedent over your own life's ambitions.

Thank you.

TABLE OF CONTENTS

Chapter One: In the Beginning…
9

Chapter Two: The Kidney Sweepstakes
12

Chapter Three: Testing, Testing, Testing
15

Chapter Four: The First Hint of Impending Disaster: My First Experience at Chicago Hopeless
20

Chapter Five: "Yo! Mama!"
26

Chapter Six: Disappointment Is Just Another Word for Pain
30

Chapter Seven: Wait, and Wait Some More
32

Chapter Eight: Chicago, Chicago
36

Chapter Nine: Fever
40

Chapter Ten: Take Two Aspirin, Drink Plenty of Fluids, Then Call Me in the Morning
45

Chapter Eleven: The Skunk Pills
50

Chapter Twleve: The Big "C"
52

Chapter Thirteen: This Is Really Starting to *Bug* Me!
56

Chapter Fourteen: "Hey! Where are you going with that cadaver?"
58

Chapter Fifteen: Burrrrrr! Baby, It's Cold Outside!
61

Chapter Sixteen: The Power of Prayer
64

Chapter Seventeen: The Red Car
67

Chapter Eighteen: Fire!
70

Chapter Nineteen: Back to "Chicago Hopeless"
73

Chapter Twenty: Two Wrights Can Make a Wrong
76

Chapter Twenty-One: Rise and Shine!
78

Chapter Twenty-Two: "Help! I can't breathe!"
84

Chapter Twenty-Three: "Water? Please! I need water!"
88

Chapter Twenty-Four: Eureka!
94

Chapter Twenty-Five: When the Going Gets Tough, the Tough Keep Going, and Going, and Going…
99

Chapter Twenty-Six: "Now you're trying to kill my sister!"
102

Chapter Twenty-Seven: Betty Is Released from the Hospital from Hell
104

Chapter Twenty-Eight: When It Rains, It Pours
107

Chapter Twenty-Nine: On a Wing and a Prayer
109

CHAPTER ONE

IN THE BEGINNING . . .

This is a story about three sisters. It is a story about family love and devotion. It is the story of a quest. It was a quest for life, liberty, and the pursuit of a healthy kidney so that life and liberty could follow for one of the sisters. It was not an easy quest; in fact, it was darn right almost an impossible quest. It encompassed innumerable sacrifices, inconveniences, insurmountable obstacles, and an impossible journey.

I am the youngest of three sisters and one brother. I say that because it always irritated my other two sisters to hear that. Lois is the oldest; she is sixty-something. Lois and her husband, Vince, have three adult children and live in Plymouth, Michigan. Betty, not Elizabeth but Betty, is the middle sister; she was sixty-something, divorced with three adult children, and lived in Danville, Illinois. I am Shirley, and I was fifty-something. I have two adult children, and I live in Eau Claire, Wisconsin. We did have a brother who passed away when he was forty-something; he lived in Beulah, Michigan. My brother's widow and daughter still live there, and his two sons are married and live out of state.

Our brother's name was Roger; he was born between Lois and Betty. I will not go into why he died; I assure you it was of natural causes. All right, he had a coronary. A lot of the men in our family seem prone to heart trouble. I can say that it has nothing whatsoever to do with the women in the family. In fact, if the men listened to the women more, they would probably lead longer, healthier lives. Anyway, I am digressing from the original intent of this story.

It has fallen upon my shoulders to document this odyssey for posterity's sake and for the sanity of the rest of my family. Why me? I guess it is because I am the closest thing we have to a writer in the family. I once had a short story published. All right, it was a children's story, but at least I can say I was published. Therefore, it is up to me to tell this tale.

How and when did all this begin? I believe Betty was born with only one functioning kidney. Betty never did anything in life halfway or, for that matter, the right way. We nicknamed her "Hurricane" at a very early age. Why "Hurricane"? She learned to run first, walk second. She has absolutely no patience and just dives right into whatever life has in store for her. She usually does this without first looking to see if there are any obstacles blocking her path. Her life story is another book.

Let us just say that she only had one functioning kidney and that, later in life, that one remaining kidney decided it'd had enough and quit. The reason the kidney decided to quit was because she was a diabetic. I do not believe that was the only reason the kidney decided to give up, but it is the reason for this book. If you wish to know all the details leading up to this book, then I, of course, will have to write Betty's life story in a future book. For now, let us just say that the kidney quit working and that she was in total renal failure; it is as good as any place to begin.

In June 1994, the family had gathered at my home in Eau Claire, Wisconsin, for the high school graduation of my youngest son, Eric, and the Yugoslavian exchange student who had been living with us the past year. Eric's life story (it isn't complete yet) would certainly make another good book. Perhaps, if this one sells well, I will contemplate that story next. Maybe I will become another Erma Bombeck. I will endeavor not to quit my day job as yet. But, again, I digress.

We were discussing Betty's kidney—or lack of kidneys, to be precise. Anyway, in June 1994, we were all together to celebrate Eric's coming of age. This would be the last time we, as a family, would all be together for a long time. This graduation party would be the last time our mother would get to see Betty for at least two years. Our mother lived in a nursing home in Eau Claire. She was 85 years old. Her life, which included living with me before the nursing home, would also make a good book. I promise to keep to the story.

Anyway, this was the last time we were all together for a while. In October—or was it November?—1994, Betty began to itch. I'm not talking just dry skin itching here; I mean she really *itched*! She literally scratched herself raw. This was the beginning of her renal failure. This type of itching is one of the symptoms. Even taking Benadryl, which puts me to sleep, didn't have any affect on her scratching. She was put in the hospital.

By Thanksgiving, it was apparent that she needed to have a kidney transplant. She did not want to go on the kidney dialysis machines, so she opted for a home care dialysis program. Her eyesight had failed so badly that she could be considered legally blind. She needed someone to lead her around. It was usual for her, at this time, to bump into walls and say "pardon me."

For the good of the general public, she did give up driving. Since she worked as a transcriptionist for the Danville Police Department, this was a very smart thing for her to do. It would not look good for the police department to have her running into other cars, pedestrians, and cute little animals. We once had a man in Eau Claire who hit a horse with his car...sorry, that's another story.

Anyway, she was off work for quite some time. It was time now for the family to begin testing to see who would be the lucky winner of the "kidney sweepstakes."

CHAPTER TWO

THE KIDNEY SWEEPSTAKES

In January 1995, Betty went back to work. She was able to do her dialysis (exchange) during her breaks—or was it her lunch hour? Betty was referred to a transplant specialist by her physician. The specialist decided that Betty should have a transplant as soon as possible. It was during this time that the family was to begin testing to see whose kidney would be the perfect match for Betty and who would be healthy enough and willing to give her a kidney.

Lois had decided that she was the best candidate. The reasoning behind her theory was that she did not work, have children living at home, or financially need to work outside of the home. She also figured that, even though she was the oldest, she was the healthiest. How she came to this conclusion is anybody's guess, but she was determined to be the donor.

We all had our blood type tested. We needed to be O+. There were five of us being tested: Lois, me, and Betty's three adult sons. We were all praying that Lois would be the donor. All of us, each for our own selfish reasons, wanted Lois to be the one. One good reason was that she really wanted to do this. The rest of us agreed to do this but would have rather not.

I, for one, could not afford the time away from work, as I also needed to accomodate a partially-disabled husband with multiple sclerosis. My husband was a teacher and had been planning on having surgery during the summer to correct a tremor he had acquired during the course of his illness. I will not go into the details of this or even the results of this surgery, because that is certainly another book. Maybe I should consider writing full time....Nah! To get back to the reason for this book, we all wanted Lois to be the *one*. As luck would have it, she wasn't.

Because Betty was diabetic, the donor had to match not only the blood type but also a number of antigens, whatever those may be. The potential donor had to be cross-matched with Betty to see how well they matched. To do this, six vials of blood were taken. That's right, *six!* As they are taking this blood, you begin to think that you should start feeling lightheaded. If your imagination is good enough, you do. This blood then had to be sent, by overnight express, to the laboratory in Chicago where the cross-matching is done.

Let us not forget that, of the five of us, all five are not in Chicago. Betty and her three offspring were sending blood in from Danville, Illinois. Lois had to send her blood in from Plymouth, Michigan. I sent my blood in from Eau Claire, Wisconsin.

Lois had a problem with this. Apparently, her clinic would not send it; she had to do it herself. My clinic (it is affiliated with Mayo Clinic) was very helpful and sent it in for me. Once the blood was sent in, we waited and waited and waited and waited some more. After three weeks of nail-biting waiting had gone by and numerous calls to the specialist's office in Chicago had been made, we finally got word. Lois did not match on any points. Two of Betty's sons didn't even have the right blood type. Betty's youngest son's blood matched very well, but the person who was a perfect match was…

It was me. You guessed it, yours truly. I could buy lottery tickets every day and never win a thing. I can't even win the baseball and football pools at work. Unfortunately, with my luck, or lack thereof, with odds of one out of five, I *won* the transplant lottery. Go figure.

I did what I had to do. I screamed, "*Why me?!*" I then called the specialist in Chicago and agreed to do this grand, wonderful, and noble thing. I figured it was good for blackmail for the rest of Betty's life. Looking at it that way made it more palatable. Now I had to begin a series of medical tests.

CHAPTER THREE

TESTING, TESTING, TESTING

In February, they started scheduling me for tests. Tests are an understatement. I must have had every test in the book. Not to mention a few they decided to just throw in for the heck of it. The specialist kept referring to my age. I do not believe he was referring to the fact that I was so young; I believe he was casting aspersions upon the fact that I was "over the hill." Betty kept telling me that I would like this doctor when I finally met him. So far, I had only spoken to him over the phone. At that time, I decided the man had no sense of humor at all. Perhaps it was just that he didn't appreciate my humor.

For two months, I was scheduled for one test after the other. I had so much blood drawn from me that I was afraid I would have none left for surgery. The technicians at the hospital all knew me by my first name.

I am not comfortable with being a patient. I have never had surgery of any kind. I am at my best as a hospital visitor. In fact, I am a professional hospital visitor. My husband has been in and out so many times that I have the routine down quite well. Now that I think about it, I wonder if he really does appreciate my visiting him when he is sick. He is always telling me I should go home. Perhaps I need to work on a better visitor's persona. I'll have to think on that a while. For now, let's get back to the story.

I hate pain. I would be a lousy spy. As soon as they would mention the word "torture," I would beg to tell them everything I knew and then make up what I didn't know. I am a coward. I have never been known for bravery. In fact, quite the opposite is true. My dentist has to put me on laughing gas just to clean my teeth. I am like the cowardly lion in *The Wizard of Oz*. Every time I had to go to the hospital for a test, my Ban deodorant would give out. I even switched to Degree. That also failed me.

I was a total basket case the day they scheduled me for an angiogram. This is the test where they go into the artery in your groin and stick a probe up into your kidneys. This did not sound like fun. I was scared half to death. I had to go to the surgery center of the hospital for this test. They would keep me all day. I was afraid to go. I had my son, Eric, drop me off at the hospital. I put on a brave front. I fooled everyone but myself.

They explained to me that they would numb the area and that I would feel no pain. To me, just being awake during the procedure was painful. They assured me they would give me something to relax me. Yeah, right.

They wheeled me into the room where the camera and equipment was set up. They had not yet given me anything to relax me. I was nearing panic.

When the doctor was ready to begin, I hollered, "Excuse me, doc! You have yet to give me anything to relax me."

Then he gave me a shot.

When he was again ready to begin, I hollered, "Excuse me doc. I'm not relaxed yet."

He assured me I would not feel any pain and that I should just relax. The nurse also assured me and then told me that the doctor had already made the incision. I was amazed! I had felt nothing. But I was still scared, especially since they would all leave the room after they had put that dye into me and then take the pictures. Was it radiation they feared? Why was I allowed to remain in the room with the radiation? A lot of questions kept going through my mind.

Once the test was over, the nurse in the room kept pressure on my wound for twenty minutes. I then had to lie flat for eight hours. I was taken to a room upstairs on one of the hospital floors. Ever try to eat a lunch tray of food lying flat on your back? It was a real challenge to lie flat and keep still, believe me.

The nurse was nice. She kept bringing me cans of diet Pepsi until I discovered that I was not allowed up to use the bathroom. I finally discovered, for myself, why they say hospitals store bedpans in the refrigerator. There is nothing less dignified than having to use a bedpan. Once I discovered the delights of using the hospital bedpan, I refused to drink any more liquids. By the time I was released from the hospital that evening, I was ready to explode. I had to pee so badly that it hurt! The next day I discovered a bruise on my upper thigh and groin area that made me look as though I had been hit by a Mack truck.

My last test was the Cardio Stress Test. There is a reason they refer to this as a stress test: they put you on a treadmill and run you uphill forever. At least, it seems like forever. I figure they run you until you have a heart attack or just plain run out of energy, whichever comes first. Luckily, in my case, I ran out of energy real early in the test. Also, lucky for me, I did not have a heart attack. What I did have was an asthma attack.

Did I mention that I had been having some problems with bronchial asthma? Sorry about that. I've talked about everything else, and I seem to have left out a very important plot point.

This latest problem began back in December 1994—Christmas Day to be exact. I came down with a real good case of bronchitis. It was such a good case that, at three a.m. the morning after Christmas, I found myself in the emergency room of our hospital having a very difficult time breathing.

I always get sick on Christmas Day. I don't know why this is;

perhaps it is a mental thing. Whatever it is, I usually get the flu, a cold, a rash, or some sort of malady by Christmas Morning. While everyone is oooohing and aaaahing over all their lovely gifts, I am puking, sneezing, wheezing, or coughing over mine. It tends to make me a little hesitant to see what Santa has brought on Christmas morning. I am never sick until the moment we begin the festivities. I really think I should see someone about this problem; it does not seem normal to me. Then again, I am not a normal person.

Let's get back to my trip to the emergency room. This is good, trust me. As I mentioned earlier in this literary masterpiece, my husband has MS. For those of you who are not familiar with this illness, it attacks the nervous system, which then affects the muscular control of its victim.

My husband has to walk with a cane. He should be using his wheelchair, but, because he is a *man*, and a stupid one at that, he prefers to use his cane as much as possible. When he uses his cane, he is very unstable and tends to fall over a lot. We are so used to it that we just tell him to get up and go on about our business. Sometimes this causes strange looks from people passing by. I think they consider it cruelty to a handicapped person. We just call it a "swift kick in the ass when he needs it" sort of thing.

Anyway, we walked into the emergency room. I was first through the door, I was having difficulty breathing, and I was in my nightgown. This fact in and of itself should have alerted the staff to something wrong. Instead, they took one look at my husband, who was teetering with his cane, and rushed over to him to help him into a wheelchair. They then proceeded to ask him all sorts of questions.

Meanwhile, back at the entryway, I was wheezing and turning blue. Once my husband had his fill of adoration and attention from the entire nursing staff, he mentioned that it isn't him but his wife who was in need of their administration. All eyes turned to me. I weakly waved to them and collapsed. To make a long story short (believe me, I could go on and on about this story, but that's another book), I was diagnosed with bronchitis and given medication. One of the medications was an inhaler.

During the months after Christmas, I continued to have problems with asthma attacks. The doctor assured me it could go away once my bronchitis cleared; then again, it could also be a permanent affliction. This is why, when I had the Cardio Stress Test, I had an asthma attack.

I could also tell you the story of how I got stranded two blocks from home during a day in February when it was $-20º$. I will spare you that and perhaps put it in another book.

The asthma attack did not happen as soon as I got off the treadmill. It waited until they had put me into the machine that takes the pictures. If you're claustrophobic, this machine is not a fun one to lie in. They had, again, shot some radioactive dye into my veins. I did ask the technician, since he knew me so well by now, if I would glow in the dark. He suggested we turn off the lights to see. He was a real comedian.

Anyway, while I was lying in this coffin-shaped camera, I started having problems breathing. When this happens, I panic. I cannot lie down; I need to sit up immediately! They finally saw through the window into the room they had put me that I was in some difficulty. They came in and got me out of the machine. They did allow me to use my inhaler and wait a few minutes. Those few minutes were not enough for me, but I had to finish the test before the dye left my system. Let's just say that it was one of the longest thirty minutes of my life. The test was finally completed. All of the tests were finally completed.

The test results had now been faxed to the specialist in Chicago. I had seen my doctor for a pre-op exam, and we were all set to go. We only had to wait to find out if I had passed all of these tests. Surgery was scheduled for Tuesday, March 21. It was now only a week away from the date of surgery.

CHAPTER FOUR

THE FIRST HINT OF IMPENDING DISASTER: MY FIRST EXPERIENCE AT CHICAGO HOPELESS

Calling the specialist's office and actually speaking to him is like talking to the Pope at the Vatican. It is almost impossible, and the dear doctor never returns his calls. The main reason is that his staff doesn't tell him about his calls. At least, in our situation, they never did. Surgery was scheduled a week away, and none of us had heard a word on any test results, if surgery was still a go, or even if the doctor knew we still existed.

I finally called the specialist's office and left a nasty message for him. That one, he got. He called me at work and assured me that everything looked just fine, that he was still waiting for a few more test results, but that everything was still a go. He also told me to be sure to tell his receptionist to page him whenever I wanted to talk to him. Even if he was in surgery, he would be able to talk to me. This did not sit well with me. What if he was operating on me? Would I want him talking to someone on the phone while he was trying to find my kidney? I think not!

I received a phone call from the specialist's transplant coordinator on Tuesday, March 14. Her name was Lena. I say "was" because, during the course of this chapter, you will discover that she is no longer the specialist's transplant coordinator. She was replaced by someone named Tom. We will certainly get to Tom in a later chapter. In fact, Thomas may well have a chapter of his own.

To get back to the story at hand, I received a phone call from Lena. I needed to give blood for surgery. That is not a problem usually. In this case, it was a big problem. By now, we were only one week away from surgery. Surgery was to take place in Chicago. I was in Wisconsin.

Wisconsin state law states that blood must be checked, then rechecked. The donor is also checked, then rechecked. After that, there is a seven-day waiting period before the blood can be used once it has been checked again. This means that your chances of contracting AIDS are greatly reduced. One of the tests I had to take was an AIDS test. I could not figure out why I had to be tested again before giving blood. Apparently, that is the rule, and they stick to it like glue.

We could not have the blood drawn in Wisconsin. Minnesota had the same rules. Therefore, I needed to travel to Chicago to give the blood. They scheduled me for the morning of Thursday, March 16, to go to the doctor's office, then on to the hospital. This is a six- to seven-hour drive for me. March has never been a predictable month in Wisconsin. Winter sometimes hangs on until June. I had to drive to Chicago; the blood had to be given. The specialist was so very sorry.

During all this time, we three sisters had been in constant communication via the telephone.

"Have you heard anything?" we would ask each other.

"No, have you?" would be the reply.

Remember, Betty has no patience. When God gave out patience, Betty thought the clerk said "patients" and stayed behind while everyone else followed the clerk out. To be perfectly honest, all three of us were still sitting there when the clerk left. By this time, the specialist was now referred to as The Big Cheese, The Big Cahuna, and The Jerk by the three of us. The name we chose usually denotes the mood at the time.

I was not happy to have to travel to Chicago. I left on Wednesday morning at nine a.m. I had directions, which I had gotten from Tom at the specialist's office. Tom had yet to get Lena's job. If you are from northern, rural Wisconsin, Chicago and Chicago's traffic can be a bit daunting. I had driven through Chicago a number of times on my way to Michigan. I drove around Chicago at those times, and still the traffic was horrendous. I was now heading for downtown Chicago.

I arrived at three p.m., during rush hour. Is my timing good or what? There is only one place to stay that is close to the hospital. I got off the expressway and followed the directions I had been given. I found the exit I needed and seemed to be in the right area. There were a number of hospitals in the area, and I located the specialist's office building but no hotel.

I drove around for a while and finally stopped to ask a nice lady waiting for a bus where it was. Her bus was late. She was waiting for a shuttle bus to take her to her job. It was late. She would direct me to the hotel if I would give her a ride to the bus stop in front of it. That sounded more than fair to me. Most people from the big city would not think of giving anyone a ride in inner city Chicago. I, if you remember, am from the boondocks of northern Wisconsin.

I had been told, by Tom, not to go more than three blocks beyond the hotel area. In any direction beyond those three blocks, I could find myself in a very terrifying situation. I was remembering this advice when the lady got in my car. Would she mug me? Take my brand new Pontiac Grand Am with CD player and sunroof? Was I in danger of being shot? All these thoughts rushed through my brain as we started out. I was nervous.

She directed me to take the next left turn. I did. She then told me to drive one block. I did. She told me to stop. I did. We were now in front of the hotel. I was one block away, one street over. I had passed the hotel a number of times looking for it. It looked just like all the other buildings around it. It was very well-camouflaged. The lady thanked me for the ride, and I thanked her for the directions. I sure felt dumb.

Now, this particular hotel has a monopoly. It is the *only* place to stay within the "safety zone, as we would eventually come to call it. There is no place to eat within a three-block area. If you walk, it has to be during the day, not at night. I was alone. The hotel cost $125.00 dollars a night. The restaurant located inside Inn cost just as much. No snack bar. They do have vending machines. They chargedyou $1.00 for soda pop in the vending machines, $1.25 for it in the bar.

I was stuck. It was dark. I did not dare to venture out. I could look out of my room window and see the skyline of Chicago. I will admit it was very pretty. I arrived at four-thirty p.m. I watched the last of Kato Kaylin's testimony in the OJ Simpson trial on CNN. I called home to let them know I had arrived. I ventured down to dinner, which I considered highway robbery, and ate a very expense, tasteless meal. I went to bed.

The next morning, I asked for the hotel shuttle to take me to the specialist's office. I got in the shuttle; he drove one block down and dropped me off in front of the building. Again, I felt stupid. I could have walked that short a distance. I murmured something about being from out of town and not knowing my way around Chicago. The driver just looked at me.

I got out and proceeded to the third floor where the specialist's office is located. No one was in the office. It was nine a.m. Where was everyone? I stood outside the door until a young man, who resembled Carter on *ER* finally opened the door. This was Tom.

Did I mention that my sister Betty and I are addicted to watching *Chicago Hope* and *ER?* Sorry, that is also a very important plot point. We love the shows and always laugh and talk about how that just might be us. Little did we know at the time just how right we would be.

It was now nine-fifteen a.m., and Lena finally came in. Some blood was taken. It seemed as though they were always taking blood from me. The specialist finally came in around ten a.m. He talked to me for a few minutes, and then they sent me over to the hospital to have a unit blood drawn for the final cross-match and a pediatric unit of blood for surgery.

I was told to go directly to the blood bank in the hospital and present them with the little prescription paper that I had in my hand. I was then to give them the files on both Betty and me that they gave to me. They pointed out the window to the hospital building. It was three blocks away, a nice walk on a brisk March day.

I got to the hospital blood bank and immediately had problems. They had no record of me coming. I was not on their computer. I did not have a hospital card. I was left to sit while they called the doctor's office and found out what was going on. I sat waiting for over an hour. I was getting pretty hungry; it was close to lunch time, and I had eaten breakfast at six-thirty a.m.

At eleven a.m., a lady came in with two people. They were transplant people also scheduled for next week. One was the donor, and one was the recipient. They were there to give their final cross-match. The head of the blood bank pointed me out to this lady.

The lady was an RN and the head of the kidney transplant unit at the hospital. From here on out, we referred to the hospital as "Chicago Hopeless." The head of the transplant unit we now refer to as "Stormin' Norman." She was fantastic.

She got on the phone to the specialist's office and to Lena. I was in the other room, but I could hear the conversation clearly. "Why is this poor woman here all the way from Wisconsin?" She reamed the doctor royally. She made no bones about the fact that Lena screws up regularly. She was a regular fire eater. I was proud to be of the female persuasion and listen to a fellow sister give someone hell.

Apparently, Lena did not tell the hospital that I was coming; they had no appointments set up for me. Lena had given me the impression that everything was all settled and that they were expecting me. Stormin' Norman took care of everything.

She sent me out to have some lunch and even gave me directions to a Kentucky Fried Chicken right on campus, just behind the hospital. She told me that I could relax and have a nice lunch and that, when I came back, everything would be ready for me. I told her that I needed to drive back to Eau Claire that day. She was very sorry that all this had happened. She assured me that they did not usually screw up in this manner and that they were one of the best hospitals for transplants. I was relieved to hear that since, so far, I had not been impressed with the place. I then left for lunch.

CHAPTER FIVE

✺

"YO! MAMA!"

Chicago is referred to as the Windy City. This is certainly true. It is usually windy there. In March, it is cold and windy. Chicago is located in America's midwest, known as the Heartland of America. I prefer to refer to Chicago as the Armpit of America's Heartland.

The people are rude, they drive like maniacs, they could care less if they run you off the road, and they are just unpleasant and unhappy people. In this beautiful city on the lake they put so many different types of people that it amazes me that it has survived this long without everyone killing each other. Perhaps it is only me who feels this way. After all, I come from rural Wisconsin where the most dangerous thing that could happen to you is to throw your back out slipping on a cow pie.

I am not a timid person. I can take care of myself. I did not always live in rural Wisconsin. I was born in Detroit, Michigan, which is even worse than Chicago. I have lived in St. Louis, Missouri, Danville, Illinois, and Grand Rapids, Michigan. Grand Rapids,

Michigan, is not a small town. When we moved to Eau Claire, Wisconsin, I went through culture shock in getting used to the rural mentality of the inhabitants of Eau Claire. I survived that and decided that it was at least peaceful. Anyway, I was now in Chicago and hungry.

I decided that Kentucky Fried Chicken sounded very appetizing for lunch. I walked over to the building that had that restaurant and a sandwich shop. I ordered my meal, sat down, read part of my book, and just relaxed. After an hour, I decided to venture back to the hospital to be there when they had asked me to return.

I left the restaurant, which is located under one of those things they refer to in Chicago as an EL train. These above-ground subways carry all sorts of people. I am not sure that some of these people are really human. One such person decided to get off this train and come down to the outside of the restaurant just as I was leaving it. This was not a smart thing for him to do. I was in a bad mood. My day had been a lousy one so far, and all I wanted to do was get in my car and leave this place. I also had a headache. This person had the nerve to stand in front of me and say, "Yo! Mama! You got some money so I can eat?"

From the way he looked—he had these dread-lock things hanging from his head—he used drugs more than food. He made me angry. I work hard for my money, and there is never enough of it. My one extravagance was my brand-new, *red*, Pontiac Grand Am. What money I had on me was mine. I worked for it. I earned it. He did not deserve any of it.

I began to tell him this and all about the social injustice that I felt was troubling this world and people like him. I also told him that I was not his mother, and proceeded to tell him about what I thought his parentage might be. I did all this while poking my finger in his chest. He just kept stepping backwards, and I just kept yelling at him. By this time, we had attracted a bit of a crowd. When the young man's legs came in contact with a concrete bench his momentum carried him backward over it.

I ended my social speech to this scum of society by placing my foot upon his chest and saying, "I may be from a small farming community in Northern Wisconsin, but I am sure not taking any *shit* from an *asshole* like you."

I bowed to the applause and then left him lying there on the sidewalk.

I was definitely ready to go home. I did not want to hang around this place any longer than I had to. I headed to the hospital in a very foul mood, and I was not going to take any more crap from them, either. When I got to the hospital, I found Stormin' Norman waiting for me with the proper paperwork, cards, and so on. I proceeded to the second floor for an EKG. I then went back to the blood bank and gave a pediatric unit of blood. It was now three p.m., and I had to report back to the doctor's office.

Once back at the doctor's office, I proceeded to tell Tom of my encounter with the dread-locked whatever he was. I also told him exactly what I felt of his town and his hospital, none of which were nice. The specialist came out, and I told him the same thing. I told him the hospital was worse than any of the episodes I have even seen on *Chicago Hope*.

The doctor had a puzzled look on his face; he did not know what a *Chicago Hope* was. Tom explained to him that it was a television show. He also explained to him about *ER*, which was also a favorite of Betty and me. The doctor apparently did not watch TV. The doctor thought it best if perhaps Betty and I did not watch these shows until surgery was over.

It was now four p.m., and I was finally free to go home. I did. It was, once again, rush hour. Oh, well.

We were scheduled for surgery on Tuesday, March 21. It was now Thursday evening, and I had a six- to seven-hour drive ahead of me to get back home. I also was expected at work the next morning. I did make it back in one piece.

On Friday morning, Lena called me to tell me to be sure and bring all my X-rays with me.

"What X-rays?" I asked.

She told me to go to the hospital and get all the X-ray pictures that they had taken. I then had to take more time off from work to go to the hospital and ask them for all of my X-rays. It was lucky for me that they had them. I now had a large, heavy envelope full of X-ray film to add to my luggage.

A friend from work joined my husband and me for a farewell dinner that evening. I received good wishes from all my co-workers and left, ready to head for Chicago again.

CHAPTER SIX

DISAPPOINTMENT IS JUST ANOTHER WORD FOR PAIN

Late Friday evening, after my husband and I had retired for the night, I received a phone call from Betty. She was upset, angry, and hurting. They were postponing surgery. An antibody had shown up in her blood during the last cross match. The doctor did not want to proceed until he knew what it was. They wanted us to do another cross-match to see if it still showed up. If not, they would reschedule surgery.

I, too, was very disappointed. I had finally gotten my mind set and ready for this. Betty needed my kidney, and she needed it as soon as possible. I was also angry that the doctor did not call me personally to tell me but left my poor sister to do it.

We were sent another kit to take to our respective clinics to have the blood drawn again. We did this and had it sent overnight again. We waited and waited and waited but heard nothing from The Jerk (doctor). We called him and got no return calls. We were beside ourselves.

Finally, Betty called and said that it was still showing up and that they would not go through with the surgery for fear of a rejection. Most of the other doctors on the team felt it was safe to go ahead with surgery. This doctor was cautious. He did not want me, because of my age, to lose a kidney for nothing. He would rather wait and be sure. He had yet to call and talk to me personally about this.

All this time, Betty had been giving blood each week to be tested with cadavers in the National Kidney Donor Bank. She was on the list as a recipient to receive a kidney if one became available. Her youngest son, Brad, matched pretty closely, and it was a possibility they would try to use his. The doctor said we would wait a while and see; perhaps he might use me in six months.

Now I was angry. I still had not heard a word from the doctor. I called his office and demanded to talk to him. I told them to page him. I was mad. They paged him, and he got on the phone. Finally, he talked to me and explained everything. We just had to go on about our lives as usual.

Waiting had become a way of life for Betty and for all of us. Betty was getting weaker, and she was getting depressed. She just wanted to get it over with. She wanted a normal life. At least, she wanted a life as normal as she could get. That meant a life without tubing sticking out of her stomach and without bags of fluid to pour through that tubing four times a day.

Hopefully, it would mean better eyesight. Some of her vision had returned with the aid of laser surgery, but she still had problems. It was not a good situation. Here I sat with a healthy kidney, one that matched her perfectly, and they did not want to use it. I was all set to go ahead anyway, take our chances, and see.

The doctor said to wait. He was being cautious, and it is to his credit that he was. It showed that he cared about both his patients. I felt a little better knowing that I wasn't just a body part to be harvested. I felt he was really concerned and cared about both of us. But it was still a hard pill to swallow.

CHAPTER SEVEN

WAIT, AND WAIT SOME MORE

Since surgery was postponed, I had to start concentrating on my husband's upcoming surgery. By June, it was obvious that the doctor would not use me as the kidney donor. My husband and I left for the Mayo Clinic in Rochester, Minnesota, on June 4, 1995. The only thing I will say about Richard's surgery in this book is that the tremor is gone. The facts that he suffered a stroke, that I was off work for most of the summer, that he had to have extensive rehabilitation, and that, by the end of July, I finally went back to work full-time are a whole other book project for the future. It should be a good one. Watch for it at a bookstore near you. Needless to say, I had a lousy summer.

By July, the specialist had decided to start testing Brad, Betty's youngest son. By the end of August, it was determined that Brad had clinical diabetes and that his kidney would not double in size to work as two. He could not donate a kidney to his mother. Betty was back to waiting for a cadaver that matched her.

In early September, I get a call from Betty. The specialist wanted to go with my kidney again. He wanted a couple more tests done on me, just to be on the safe side. I was sick of tests. I was sick of hospitals. I was sick of doctors. By this time, I had a husband who believed that he was totally disabled and who was not even trying to get better. I was in a very bad mood, and all I needed was to have to go through major surgery myself. I, of course, said I would do it. What can I say? I'm crazy that way?

The specialist wanted another Cardio Stress Test. I refused. I'd had the cardiologist from Hell administer the first one and did not want a repeat performance. I had not had any problems with asthma since March. I did not want to have any more problems with it, period.

My personal doctor had given me a prescription of Prednisone to take for one week. I took these two weeks before the first surgery was scheduled. It had apparently worked, for I had no recurring problems with asthma. Still, I did not want to take the Cardio Stress Test again. I figured that, if I had a heart attack and died on the operating table, it would be a lot more peaceful than my life was at this point in time. I could at least rest.

It was at this time that we discovered that Lena was no longer working at the specialist's office. Why, we do not know. We have never asked. Tom was now the transplant coordinator for the specialist. He is his assistant, even in surgery. He was going to set up and schedule all of my tests. He would also let us know the date of surgery. He did.

Two weeks before we were scheduled for surgery, I got a call from Tom one morning at work to tell me that we were scheduled for surgery on September 19. I called Betty when I got home that evening and discovered that no one in the specialist's office had called her to tell her about the date of surgery. Betty waited another day, then she finally called Tom at the doctor's office. She wanted to know what would happen if she didn't show up. He apologized that no one had contacted her. This was Tom's first mistake. This should have alerted us to the possibility of more problems ahead. What can I say? We were naive.

The specialist assured me that I would be taking what they called a Cardio Lite stress Test. I asked if that was anything like a Bud Lite. Again, the man had no sense of humor. I was also scheduled for another CAT scan of my heart and kidneys. I, yet again, was shot full of radioactive material and was afraid of becoming a human light bulb.

They scheduled the tests for the first two weeks in September. I had four tests in all. I had no idea what they were all for, and, at this point, I didn't want to know. The first part of the Cardio Lite test just involved taking pictures, which they did on September 13.

It was at this time I discovered that there was indeed a treadmill involved in the test. That was the second part. This was when I figured out that the specialist had fibbed. All the "Lite" referred to was the radioactive injection of whatever it is called. They could not schedule the treadmill part of the test until the afternoon of September 15.

I was leaving on the 16th so my that son could drive me to Chicago and then drive home on Sunday. Eric was now in his second year at the local technical college, studying to become a police officer. He had to be back in town for school, which I did not want him to miss. My oldest son, Bill, was a 24-year-old restaurant manager. Bill planned to get off work and drive to Chicago on Monday evening for surgery on Tuesday. I had to be there early Monday to give blood again. Betty and I both had to do another final cross-match on Monday.

On September 12, Bill's best friend decided to end his life. We were all devastated by this news. We were also shocked by it. No one could figure out why he did it. It was a very hard week to get through. I was not only scheduled for this stress test on Friday afternoon, but I also had to attend this young man's funeral on Friday morning.

I was definitely stressed. I explained it to the cardiologist (who, by the way, was the same cardiologist from Hell that I'd had the last time) all that I had been through. I began with the way that the doctor had canceled the first surgery and told her about my summer. They were now totally sure that I had lots of stress. I got a cramp in my right calf after about six minutes of running uphill at full speed during the treadmill test. The cardiologist was kind enough to slow the treadmill down for me and then stop the test after eight minutes. She said that my heart seemed to be doing just fine.

My heart, at the moment, was not what I was concerned about. My right leg, by this time, had knotted up like some sailor's rope. I hobbled out of the hospital and headed to work for the last two hours of the work day.

I kept my fingers crossed that this time we would receive no-last minute phone calls. We did. At four on Friday, Tom called. He had Betty on the phone, so we had a conference call. I was furious.

"Don't you dare tell us we are canceled!"

"You're canceled," he replied.

He got it from both of us. We were rescheduled for Friday, September 22. Tom said that the hospital had some scheduling problems. The hospital later told us that Tom was the one who had failed to tell them that we were scheduled for surgery. He had decided on the date but had failed to schedule it at the hospital. We are now at strike two for Tom.

I decided to go to Chicago as planned since there was no way I could get there in the middle of the week. Since I was flying home, I needed my son to drive me and bring the car home. He had school during the week. My husband was totally useless and still moaning (with his head shaved, he resembled a Hare Krishna) about how life was so unfair. My son and I proceeded to continue to give him verbal kicks in the ass, it was to no avail.

Betty decided to come to Chicago on Sunday as planned so that we could visit and do some sight-seeing. Lois had decided to play mother hen and was coming with us to take care of us. She also decided to come on Sunday. We would spend a nice relaxing week together. We would relax and, if possible, do some sightseeing. What is it they say about the best laid plans of mice and men?

CHAPTER EIGHT

✹

CHICAGO, CHICAGO

Eric and I left Eau Claire on the morning of Saturday, September 17, at seven a.m. Just the thought of being shut up in a car for more than six hours with Eric was frightening. His taste in music and my taste in music are so far apart that I sometimes wonder if the kid was switched at birth. We did manage to arrive in Chicago at three p.m. By the time we checked into the University Inn, our nerves and tempers were way past any sort of tolerance zone.

We did manage to ask the receptionist at the hotel if there were any places within walking distance where we could get a good cheap meal. The other attendant at the desk made some snide comment about a Burger King not too far away. The nice attendant told us that there were a number of nice places to eat just three blocks over. It was still light outside, so Eric and I headed out and found a nice place to eat.

After returning to the hotel, we decided to try to do some sightseeing on Sunday morning. We called the font desk. The shuttle bus did not run until ten a.m. on Sundays, and we had to be back at the hotel at noon to meet the rest of the family that was coming in.

These illustrious members of our family were: my sister Lois, her husband, Vince, and their daughter, Carey, my sister Betty, and her oldest son, Jeff, who was driving her into Chicago. Vince and Carey were driving back to Plymouth on Sunday evening and coming back the following weekend after surgery on Friday. My oldest son, Bill, was coming on Sunday evening because he was unable to get his schedule changed because of the funeral and because the specialist's assistant, Tom, screwed up the surgery schedule. We had found alternate accommodations at one of the dorm halls that have a room set aside for transplant families. We were unable to move into the dorm room until Monday. Betty's son Jeff had to be home on Monday evening but would be back on Thursday evening with his two brothers, Greg and Brad, for surgery on Friday.

So all of these people were to arrive at various times during the week. We would figure out how to fit everyone into a three-bedroom dorm room when the time came. Since the boys were all young, we didn't think that having to sleep in sleeping bags on the floor would harm them any.

Eric and I ordered the shuttle for ten a.m. Sunday morning and were scheduled to go to the new Navy Pier. We got up and found that they had donuts, juice, and coffee set up in the bar. We were delighted to see they had a continental breakfast.

We later discovered that the breakfast was for a visiting group of doctors there for a symposium. Oh, well, the donuts were good, and they didn't seem to notice two more people in their group. Besides, most of them didn't speak English, anyway.

The shuttle did not arrive for us until eleven. The driver said he had a flat tire. We got to the Navy Pier and literally ran up and down it. We did not have time to ride the world's largest ferris wheel, even though I had already bought tickets. Eric scarfed down a brat, hotdog, and Pepsi while we were running to the end of the pier to see Lake Michigan. Eric quickly snapped a few pictures, and we ran back to the spot where the shuttle was to pick us up at eleven-thirty.

When we arrived at the hotel, Lois and her group were just arriving. We told them about the restaurants we had discovered the night before. After they checked in, we walked over to a pub and enjoyed a nice lunch.

By two p.m., Eric had left to drive back to Eau Claire, and Betty and Jeff had arrived. They had gotten lost. Betty was in a real temper. She was supposed to have done an exchange (dialysis) a couple of hours before, so her temper was not at its best.

Betty lives only two hours from Chicago, but putting her and Jeff in a car together for two hours is asking for major problems. Jeff complained that all she did was bitch the whole way. Betty claimed that Jeff couldn't find his way out of a paper bag. She once told him to stop and ask a blind man on the street for directions. She figured the blind man would know more than Jeff did.

Well, we were all finally in Chicago. Now all we had to do was call a lady named Pat at the liver transplant unit on Monday and arrange to pick up the key to the dormitory room. The dormitory room was $35.00 a day, whereas the Inn charged $68.00 a day with a medical discount.

We decided to walk over to the pub again for dinner. Betty was unable to walk that far. Because of her diabetes, she had a circulation problem in one leg. She had to wear a three-pound brace on that leg and a special shoe. Walking that far in her condition was out of the question. The Inn had no wheelchairs, so we asked for the shuttle. Vince and Carey left for Plymouth at four p.m. The rest of us hopped into the Inn shuttle and went to the pub.

We told the driver to pick us up at five-thirty p.m. We had a very nice meal and relaxed. At five-twenty, we went outside to wait for the shuttle. At five-forty-five, he still had not arrived. At six, I walked back to the hotel to inquire about the shuttle and why it had not picked up our party at the restaurant. The shuttle driver forgot to write us down on his schedule. I then lost my temper, and the shuttle was sent to retrieve my family. At six-fifteen, the shuttle finally arrived at the hotel carrying Betty and Lois. Jeff had already gotten tired of waiting and walked back.

At ten p.m., Bill arrived with his friend Craig. It was Craig's truck that they used to travel to Chicago. Craig is a wonderful chef and a good friend of Bill's. He came to Rochester and visited with us while Richard was in the hospital there; I had seen him at the funeral on Friday just before I left for Chicago. He is a real cutie. He is the type of young man whose cheeks you want to pinch when he smiles and you see those adorable dimples.

Now Jeff, Craig, and Bill are in one room while Betty, Lois, and I are in the other room. We all settled down for a nice, restful sleep. We were glad that we were only staying in the Inn Sunday night. By Monday, we would move into the dormitory. We were all set, or so we thought.

CHAPTER NINE

✸

FEVER

Monday morning, at eight-thirty a.m., Betty called Pat at the liver transplant office. She was not there yet but would call us back as soon as she got in. At nine, I called the specialist's office, and they told me to come to the office in the afternoon. At nine-oh-five, Betty again tried to call the lady at the liver transplant office. This time, they page her and she called us back. We were beginning to wonder about this place. She told us to go over to the clinic across the street from the hospital and ask for directions to Blue 53. They would then direct us to her office, which was in Blue 53. We called downstairs about using the shuttle. "No problem," they said, "come right down." We did. We also checked out.

While we were checking out, we discovered that they were trying to get us to pay the wrong bill. There were a lot of room service charges on the bill of one of the rooms. We never used room service. We finally were able to get them to see that they were giving us the bill for the wrong room numbers. It took a while, but we finally got it all straightened out. But, by then, the shuttle had disappeared.

It was now after eleven a.m. While we were waiting for the shuttle, the specialist's office called me. I took the call in the entryway of the hotel. The doctor wanted to know what I was doing and where I was going. I told him we were going to pick up the key to the dormitory room and move in.

He had news for us. Surgery had now been rescheduled to Thursday afternoon. They were unable to get the team together for Friday morning, so they would do our surgery on Thursday afternoon. Also, Tom, the specialist's assistant, forgot to tell us to be at the hospital that morning for the final cross-match and for me to give blood. He asked us to go to the hospital as soon as we got settled in the dorm.

We decided not to wait for the shuttle. Bill and Craig took all of our luggage in the pick-up truck. Lois, Betty, Jeff, and I got into Betty's car and drove over to the clinic to get the key. Bill and Craig were following us in the truck; we turned, and they didn't. Now Bill and Craig were lost, along with all of our luggage. We arrived at the clinic, and Jeff dropped us off and tried to park the car.

Inside the clinic, I asked the receptionist for Blue 53. She told us to follow the blue line on the floor. There were five lines on the floor, all different colors. It's a good thing we weren't color blind. I saw a wheelchair behind the receptionist. I asked if we could please use it for my sister.

"Where is she going?" the receptionist asked.

"We are going to Blue 53, the liver transplant unit," I replied.

She now believes that Betty is getting a liver transplant and is too weak to walk. We, of course, did not correct this assumption. Lois wheeled Betty through the clinic as we followed the blue line. We felt like we were in the middle of the *Wizard of Oz* and started singing "Follow the Yellow Brick Road." We got a lot of strange stares as we traversed the hallways of the clinic.

The room we needed is at the back of the clinic and takes forever to find, but we finally made it. Lois was so tired after pushing the chair that she complained that it seemed to pull to the right. Her left shoulder hurt.

Pat was not in the office. She would be at least another ten minutes. I decided to try to find the boys. I got back to the front entrance: no truck, no car, and no boys. Coming back inside the clinic, I spotted Jeff. He had gone upstairs to the kidney transplant office, and they did not know us. I explained that we were picking the key up from a lady in the liver transplant office. I led him back to Blue 53. Still, there was no sign of Bill and Craig. Jeff never saw them, either.

Once back in Blue 53, Lois was again complaining about her shoulder and that darn wheelchair pulling to the right. Jeff told her it was because the left-hand break had been on. We all thought that was hilarious.

Finally, Pat arrived and took us over to the dormitory. We asked Pat for the use of a wheelchair, but she said that they didn't have any to lend out. In fact, it is hard to get one anywhere on the medical campus. We decided to keep the one we had (it said "property of" and the name of the hospital on the side).

The dormitory is in the second building behind the clinic. We were on the second floor. One of the bedrooms was unusable. There was a gapping hole in the ceiling where it had leaked. The leak had been fixed, but the ceiling had not.

Betty and I had to get to the hospital for our blood tests and pre-admit testing. Lois went with Pat on a tour of the facilities. Betty and I took off for the hospital with the stolen wheelchair. Jeff went to look for the boys and to move us into the dormitory while we were at the hospital.

We finally found the boys as we were walking to the hospital. They had been all over the clinic looking for us and were told to check the hospital. They found us, and we sent them to the dormitory to move us in. We decided to have lunch in the hospital cafeteria. The boys would meet us there as soon as they moved our luggage into the dorm. We had a nice, relaxing lunch then Betty and I headed to the blood bank.

At the hospital, we found Stormin' Norman pacing in front of the blood bank. The doctor's office told her that we would be there at eleven. It was now one-thirty p.m. Again, the specialist's assistant, Tom, had screwed up. We were not amused. Lois and Pat arrived after their lunch and tour.

Betty and I got our pre-admit papers filled out, and they drew blood from us. We were scheduled for chest X-rays and EKGs. I was scheduled to give blood for surgery, so I went to the blood bank first. Betty and Lois waited outside for Betty to get her blood and urine tested. Inside the blood bank, I was all set to go.

There seemed to be one small problem. They discovered that I was running a fever of 101.4 degrees. I could not give blood. The fever could be a problem, and surgery could get canceled. They sent me on to get my chest X-ray and EKG anyway. They kept asking me if I felt sick. I kept saying no. They would know when I saw the doctor the next day and they had the blood and urine tests back. Meanwhile, I was to relax, drink plenty of fluids, and eat ice chips.

I went back to the dorm to rest while Betty finished her tests. When Betty came back, she was alone. Lois had taken the wheelchair back. I asked why. We still needed that chair to get to the doctor's office the next day, not to mention to go out to eat that night. Lois came back, minus the wheelchair. Jeff headed back to Danville.

The rest of us decided to get in Craig's truck and go to one of the restaurants we had finally discovered for dinner. It was six p.m. The restaurant is three and a half blocks from the dormitory, but Betty could not walk that far. It was too cold outside to ride in the back of the truck, and they said that I couldn't because I had a fever.

Craig's truck was a little truck, but it did have a very little back seat. Craig is not a small young man. Craig and Lois squeezed into the back seat of the truck. I hugged the gear shift in the front seat, and Betty squeezed into the passenger seat. My son, Bill, is 6 feet, 9 inches tall. In order for Lois and Craig to fit in the back seat, he had to have the front seat all the way forward. The poor boy was driving the truck with his knees up under his chin.

We decided on an Italian restaurant, and this marks our last meal in a restaurant. Bill and Craig would be going back to Eau Claire the next afternoon and that left us poor sisters without any transportation. From now on, it would be dorm or hospital food for the three of us. We were looking forward to this last meal.

We parked the truck in the lot in back of the restaurant. There was a back entrance. At least, we thought it was a back entrance. We went in and discovered that it was the kitchen. I turned to leave, but this nice Chinese man assured me that this was the entrance. I wondered for a while why a Chinese man owned an Italian restaurant, but it is Chicago after all.

We continued into the restaurant. It was dark inside after being out in the sunshine. Betty tripped on the step going down into the kitchen and broke the screw on her leg brace. It did have Velcro which wrapped around her leg, so at least it wouldn't fall off until we could get it fixed. We had a lovely meal and then piled back into the truck and went back to the dorm. We figured that this was a bad day but that it certainly can't get any worse. It could only get better, right? *Wrong!*

CHAPTER TEN

✸

TAKE TWO ASPIRIN, DRINK PLENTY OF FLUIDS, THEN CALL ME IN THE MORNING

I was a basket case. We were so close to surgery, and I had this stupid fever. Why? I didn't feel sick. It would be entirely my fault if surgery got canceled. I hardly slept that night. It was our first night in the dorm. I got one room to myself (I snore). Betty and Lois shared the remaining undamaged bedroom.

The dorm had a long hallway, or entryway, with a bathroom off this hallway. There was a turn to the left, and the kitchen and dining area were in another long hallway. One bedroom was on the right-hand side of the kitchen/dining area with one single bed, a desk, a dresser, and a TV. This TV only got NBC and CBS. Then next bedroom (mine) was just past the kitchen area with one single bed, desk, and dresser. There was no TV in this room. The last bedroom (Lois and Betty's) was just across from the second bedroom. It had two single beds, a dresser and a TV. This TV only got ABC. Each bedroom had a closet with shelves in it.

The kitchen was stocked with a refrigerator, stove, pots and pans, dishes, silverware, and a sink, which had cupboards over it. We, of course, needed to supply the food. There was a small round table with three chairs on which we ate and played cards and scrabble. There was also a telephone on that table. The telephone worked but could only receive calls. We had to go down to the lobby to use the public pay phones when we needed to make a call.

We took the chairs from the kitchen table into the bedroom to watch TV. We had to move our chairs from room to room, depending on which channel we wanted to watch. Since it was Monday night, the premier episode of that season's *Chicago Hope* was airing. Betty and I couldn't wait to see it. Hopefully, I would relax, my fever would go away, and, by tomorrow, all would be well again. I bought some bottles of Evian water and had been drinking it until my kidneys were literally floating. At ten, we went to bed. I tossed and turned all night, worrying about the next day.

Tuesday morning, September 19, dawned bright and sunny. Betty took the first shower. Well, Betty tried to take the first shower. She hollered out to Lois and me, "How do I turn this thing on?" We went in to take a look. There was Betty, stark naked, Lois, and me, all in this tiny bathroom trying to figure out how to turn on the shower. None of us could figure it out. There was no handle to pull or turn. The shower head had no lever or knobs to turn. We could find nothing on the spigot to turn the dang thing on with either.

Betty took her shower using a small paper cup we found in the kitchen. Lois and I went without. I was a wreck without my morning shower. My hair was a greasy mess and stuck up all over my head. I did the best I could to look presentable, which didn't seem to help much.

We went down to the basement of the building where the student housing is located. We asked the young man there how to turn on the shower. We must have looked like complete country hicks because nobody in that office was able to keep a straight face while he explained it to us. We felt like complete idiots after he did explain it to us. You just gently pull down on a ring located on the faucet; the shower then comes on.

We were late; we had to call the doctor's office and then eat breakfast. We called the doctor's office and were told to be there by ten a.m. We ate breakfast in the student commons cafeteria. We would eventually grow to hate that cafeteria.

Lois and I then went to the clinic across the street to steal a wheelchair. We went in the back entrance by orthopedics, which was next to Blue 53. We walked all the way through the building back to the reception area to get a wheelchair. There were no wheelchairs. There were plenty of signs that said, "Do Not Remove From Bldg.," but no wheelchairs.

We asked the receptionist for one. She said they were all being used. We explained that our sister was out in the car and needed one to get in the building. She asked where we were parked, and I told her. She said that was real close to Blue 53 and asked if she could walk that far. I lied. I said she was too weak and sickly. The receptionist called orthopedics to see if they had one so that we could get our dear, sick sister out of the car and into the liver transplant office. Orthopedics had a chair. We turned, ready to hightail it back through the building, and ran smack into Stormin' Norman. She wanted to know what we girls were up to.

I said, "Stealing a wheelchair."

She never even batted an eye. She said that sounded good to her. She wanted to know how I felt. I said I felt just fine. She thought that was unusual since my urine tests showed a bladder infection. We told her that we were on our way to the doctor's office so that he could check me over but that we had to go back to the student union with our soon-to-be stolen wheelchair to get Betty. Stormin' Norman wanted to know why we had left Betty at the student union.

"It was as far as we could get her," we explained.

She wished us luck and hoped that the doctor put me on an antibiotic that would do the trick so surgery would not be canceled. We ran back to orthopedics. The girl there told us to go back to a room by the coat rack and borrow a chair from there. It was the only one there. We took it, slowly rolled it outside, and then ran like hell for the student union. We then put Betty in the chair and left the student union by another exit so we wouldn't be spotted. We did eventually return the chair but not to the clinic building. I will explain that in a later chapter.

We were now on our three-block walk to the doctor's office. Betty had always seen the doctor when he visited Danville. Betty had never been to the doctor's Chicago office before. I led the way; Lois pushed the wheelchair, this time with both brakes off. We had a couple of close calls crossing the street. Pedestrians do not seem to have the right of way in Chicago. In fact, handicapped people must really have a hard time getting around in this big, unfeeling metropolis. After cussing a few drivers out, we finally made it in one piece to the doctor's office.

The doctor put the three of us in his office on the sofa. We looked like the three monkeys: hear no evil, see no evil, speak no evil. Betty coughed. The doctor immediately ran into the room, "Who coughed?" Betty and I both pointed to Lois.

The doctor took me in to examine me. My pulse was 120, and my blood pressure was very high. This was odd; I had never had a problem with blood pressure before. I wondered if it could be because of all the stress we had encountered since arriving in Chicago. My fever was still up. He gave me some pills to take, told me to drink plenty of fluids, and chew ice chips.

He then sent us back to the dorm to rest. We were to come back on Wednesday morning; at least, I was to come back. Surgery was being postponed, not canceled, until my fever and infection were both gone. At least we were still going to do the surgery; we didn't know when, but we were still going to go for it. I felt a little better after that. The doctor told us to stay in the dorm and stay out of trouble.

When we left his office, he wanted to know where we had gotten the wheelchair.

Before I could think, I said, "We stole it."

I mentioned that, if the campus police came looking for us, he did not know where we were staying. We then left him with a very puzzled and troubled look on his face.

CHICAGO HOPELESS

We went back to the dorm and played rummy for the rest of the afternoon. We ate lunch and dinner in the cafeteria in the student union. We went to bed at ten. I worried all night again. Would things finally work out? Would my fever be gone in the morning?

CHAPTER ELEVEN

THE SKUNK PILLS

I really should explain about the anti-rejection medication that Betty had to start taking before surgery. They are called Cyclosporine. They are humongous pills. They also stink! Stink is an understatement. You needed a gas mask to give these things to her. Your eyes watered, your stomach churned, your nose wrinkled, and the whole dorm room smelled like a skunk had decided to spray the place. These pills are horrible.

Betty hates to take pills. She has a very difficult time swallowing pills. To give her medication, she must have a diet Pepsi (a whole one just for an aspirin) to drink. You must also threaten her into taking the pills. She tends to gag a bit, even taking aspirin.

Not only are Cyclosporine pills stinky, but they are also very large. They would be very difficult for even a horse to swallow. Getting Betty to take these pills became a nightly chore. She was worse than any two-year-old ever thought of being. She had to take eight of these pills, three times a day. This was not an easy job to accomplish, believe me.

CHICAGO HOPELESS

Lois usually got the job of giving Betty her medicine. She is the nursemaid, remember? We would all hold our noses during this ritual and beg Betty to swallow them as soon as possible, before we all passed out. Then Lois would scrub her hands for the next half hour just to try to get the smell out of them.

Betty had started taking the medication a week before surgery. She had to continue taking it when surgery was postponed. So, you can imagine who was cursed every time it came time for the skunk pills to be administered. You guessed it! Little ol' me!

CHAPTER TWELVE

✹

THE BIG "C"

Wednesday morning, September 20, 1995, dawned bright and sunny. I, on the other hand, was not. I still had a fever. At nine a.m., I walked the three and half blocks over to the doctor's office. They needed to check my vital signs again. I hate the sight of a thermometer, and, even more, I hate the sight of a blood pressure cuff. I was so nervous. I just knew I was going to be the reason surgery was called off.

At the doctor's office, it was discovered that I was still running a fever of over 100 degrees. They took my blood pressure, and it was still very high. My heart rate was over 120.

Tom called the doctor; he was in his car traveling to some location in this huge metropolis. The doctor asked to speak to me. When I got on the phone, he said that my fever was still too high and that he was concerned about my blood pressure and heart rate. I kept trying to convince him that I was just nervous about the surgery getting canceled again.

He told me that he was going to make an appointment for me to see some big-wig cardiologist. He was also scheduling me for a kidney ultrasound and a triple renal scan. He was concerned that I might be starting to experience renal failure. He told me that surgery had been rescheduled for next Tuesday if all the tests came back all right and if the cardiologist said that it was safe to operate on me.

I was to return to the dorm to await a telephone call from Tom so that he could give me the times of my appointments. Before I left the doctor's office, Tom had me pee in a cup so they could check my urine to see how the bladder infection was doing. I head back to the dorm very dejected.

On my walk back to the dorm building, I stopped at the little store in the student union and bought a thermometer. I decided to start checking my temperature myself. I was beginning to believe that my temperature, blood pressure, and heart rate all had something to do with Tom and/or the doctor's office. When I was there, I had a fever and palpitations. I don't think it was lust for Tom's body, but, hey, who knows?

When I arrived at the dorm room, it was to discover a drywall man fixing the ceiling in the bedroom with a hole in the ceiling. Betty was shut up in the bedroom that had the other TV. She was giving herself dialysis. In order for her to do her dialysis, she needed a sterile environment. This certainly did not look like a clean environment. There was plaster dust all over everything. The repair man was working away. He was drilling, sanding, and pounding away in the bedroom, oblivious to the fact that we had a very sick person trying to give herself her home dialysis in one of the other bedrooms. The poor man's pants seemed to want to fall below the beer belly he had, so we were constantly seeing a definite "crack in the moon." He assures us that it would only be another hour or two before he would be out of our hair. Well, he might be out of our hair, but the plaster dust would certainly remain there until we could all shower again.

During all of this, the building maintenance man came by. Our toilet leaked, so he was going to try to fix it. No luck. They needed to replace the toilet. Lois told them they would have to wait till after

Tuesday to do this, since that is when we were scheduled for surgery. No one would be in the room on Tuesday, so they said they would come back then. Meanwhile, they said that they had temporarily stopped the leak.

During all of the pounding and sanding, Tom called to tell me to go over to the hospital to do the triple renal scan. When I was done with that test, I was to call them, and they would tell me when my appointment with the cardiologist would be and when I would be scheduled for the ultrasound. I left Betty and Lois to deal with the entire crew of fix-it men and trekked the three and a half blocks over to "Chicago Hopeless."

The triple renal scan was really an easy test. They injected some dye into my veins, and I sat in a special chair while they spent forty minutes taking pictures of my kidneys and bladder. They watched the dye travel through the kidneys and into the bladder. Before the test, they had me drink a large glass of water, wait a bit, then pee. Once my bladder was empty, they injected me with the dye and begin the filming. This was the second triple renal scan I have had done. The technician was real nice; he told me that everything was looking great. No problems, no kidney stones. It looked as though I had two very healthy kidneys. I could have told him that. I had already had one done and found out the very same thing then.

When the test was done I found a pay phone and called the doctor's office. I had to run (and I mean run!) over to the doctor's office building. The cardiologist appointment was in fifteen minutes, and he was located two floors above our doctor's office. I quickly called the dorm to tell my partners in crime that I had to go to the cardiologist's office. They told me they were on their way to the doctor's office building, too. Betty needed to give more blood.

Now the weather had changed for the worse. It was now overcast, windy, and raining. Lois had to push Betty the three and a half blocks to the doctor's office, trying not to tip her out of the chair at all the intersections. I, in the mean time, ran like *hell* to the doctor's office building to get to my appointment.

Now I was really nervous. Here was some fancy heart specialist who was going to examine me. Talk about a fast heart rate. My heart was literally pounding now. The specialist came in and examined me. He was very nice. He told me to relax. Yeah, right!

After asking me hundreds of questions, listening to my heart, and examining me, he decided that I was just very nervous. *No kidding, Sherlock!* We actually had to pay this guy to tell the doctor what I had been trying to get through his head for the last two days. I leave the doctor's office very relieved. He assured me that there was nothing wrong with my heart, my heart rate, or my blood pressure. He believed that everything would show up normal once we were actually having surgery. When my anxiety level dropped, so would my blood pressure and heart rate. It took a $200.00-an-hour specialist to tell them what I already knew. Go figure!

Once I got back at the dorm, I discovered that Lois had browbeaten housekeeping into coming up and giving the dorm room a good cleaning. She told them that Betty could not be in the room with all of that plaster dust, that she would become very ill. Fearing that they would somehow be responsible if Betty died of an infection, housekeeping was cleaning the room when I return. Things were starting to look up. Finally, it looked like everything was going to work out. Or were they?

CHAPTER THIRTEEN

✺

THIS IS REALLY STARTING TO *BUG* ME!

It was now Thursday morning, September 21, 1995. I got up and took my temperature: 99.6 degrees. Well, at least it was coming down. I headed into the bathroom to empty my full bladder. My feet got wet while I was sitting on the stool. Guess that leak they fixed wasn't fixed, after all. We wrapped paper towels around the base of the toilet again. We had to remember to wear shoes and not to be in stockinged feet while using the toilet unless we wanted wet feet. Now I discovered another problem. We were out of toilet paper. I scrambled around, looking for a Kleenex box; thank goodness I found one.

On the way back from breakfast, we stole some toilet paper from one of the bathrooms in the student union. We were turning into petty thieves. This town certainly has an effect on people—and not a nice effect either.

We decided to relax and play some cards. At nine, we got a telephone call from the doctor's office. Betty had to go back over to the doctor's office to give some more blood. Apparently, the hospital did the wrong test on the last tube she gave them. They performed a pregnancy test. Is this place for real? We decided that perhaps we should buy some yellow sticky notes so that we could start labeling the parts of our bodies for them so that they would know who the donor was and who the recipient was. We trekked the three and a half blocks to the doctor's office again.

Upon arriving at the dorm building, we noticed a sign on all the elevator doors. "Dorm Building Will Have Exterminators from 10 a.m.-3 p.m. on Friday; Sorry for Any Inconvenience This May Cause You." First we had to contend with plaster dust; now it looked like we would have to inhale noxious bug spray, too!

We stop at the Housekeeping department to tell them that the toilet was leaking again and that we were out of toilet paper. (We were now even out of what we stole; we were getting desperate!) The lady on duty there took Lois into a back storage room. Betty and I stood around for about ten minutes, wondering what was going on. Finally, there came Lois, dragging a very *large*, and I mean *huge*, plastic bag full of towels, extra blankets, toilet paper, Kleenex, cleaning solution, soap, and God knows what else. She literally dragged the bag up to the second floor and into our room. Well, at least we didn't steal it this time.

CHAPTER FOURTEEN

✸

"HEY! WHERE ARE YOU GOING WITH THAT CADAVER?"

It was now a little before the noon hour, and Betty needed to give herself dialysis. While sitting there, she noticed that, because surgery had been postponed, she did not have enough solution bags to make it until Monday when we were to check into the hospital. Now what? We called the doctor's office. "Hey, Tom, guess what?" He told us to come over so they could give us a prescription for some more solution.

Luckily, Brad and Greg (Betty's boys) arrived for an overnight visit. They had the time off because surgery was supposed to be that day, so they decided to come up and visit with us, anyway. We would need their truck to get the boxes of solution back to the dorm. Of course, the truck was parked in the hospital parking ramp, which was four blocks away. We all decided to go over to "Chicago Hopeless" to eat lunch in the cafeteria since I had an appointment for an ultrasound later in the afternoon. After we ate, Betty, Lois, Brad, and

Greg went over to the doctor's office, and I headed over to radiology for my Kidney Ultrasound.

While I was having my Ultrasound, the other group of misfits was having a bit of a problem getting Betty's prescription filled. The pharmacy in the doctor's office building could not fill such a large order; only the hospital pharmacy could handle that, but the hospital did not have an outpatient pharmacy. They had a pharmaceutical department located in the basement next to pathology and the autopsy room. It is pretty spooky down there. The four misfits were now surrounded by dead bodies. The hospital told them that they could not fill such prescriptions for outpatients.

Brad lost his temper, threatened the poor defenseless man with great bodily harm, and told him to call the transplant unit. Stormin' Norman made sure that the order was filled, and the head of the pharmacy department personally wheeled the loaded cart out to Brad's truck in the parking ramp and loaded it up with boxes of solution.

I met everyone in the cafeteria for an afternoon snack. Brad and Greg left us three sisters in the cafeteria to relax with a nice soda while they took the solution over to the dorm. The truck had to be parked in the hospital parking ramp so that it didn't get stolen or ripped apart and sold for parts.

We decide to wait for the boys to come back after parking the truck so that we could all walk over to the dorm together. When the boys get back, we all headed out for our trek back to the dorm. It was now very cold and rainy out.

Brad threw his jacket over Betty's head to keep her from getting wet and started to run with her in the wheelchair back over to the dorm. The two of them looked like something from the movie *Weekend at Bernie's*. Greg, Lois, and I followed behind at a much slower pace while Brad was running across a busy street with Betty, her head fully covered, sitting in the wheelchair.

Greg hollered out at the top of his lungs, "*Hey!* Where are you going with that cadaver?"

All of the pedestrians stopped to watch Brad running like mad, pushing a wheelchair with what looked like a dead body sitting in it. I decided to distance myself from this group of obviously *sick* people. I did not want anyone to know that I was even remotely associated with them, let alone related to them.

CHAPTER FIFTEEN

❋

BURRRRRR! BABY, IT'S COLD OUTSIDE!

It was now Friday morning, September 22, 1995. Brad and Greg took off for Danville early in the morning. I took my temperature, and it was normal! Betty needed to go to the doctor's office again to give blood; I decided to stay at the dorm so that they wouldn't try to take my temperature or blood pressure.

It was getting very cold outside. Lois and I put Betty into a pair of my heavy jeans, a turtleneck, and one of my extra warm sweatshirts. Betty put on Lois' hooded sweatshirt jacket to cover her head then put her jacket on over it. Lois and I wrapped a blanket around Betty in the wheelchair, and Lois starts pushing her in the wheelchair on the three-and-a-half-block trek to the doctor's office.

They had only been gone about ten minutes when Tom called. He told me that I needed to come to the office, too. We were to give blood for the final cross-match that day. Since surgery was postponed, they needed to do another cross match. I put on my jacket and went out into the windy, rainy day to meet Betty and Lois at the doctor's. Once I got to the doctor's office, Tom tried to take my temperature and blood pressure.

I fought him off. I keep screaming, "*No, no!*"

The patients in the waiting room were wondering what was going on, a few possibly even left. I refused to let him take my temperature or my blood pressure. I told him that it was all his his fault that they kept going up and that I wanted him to leave me alone. Meanwhile, out in the waiting room, my two siblings calmly sat looking at a magazine while more patients began to get nervous. I do allow him to take the blood needed for the cross-match.

Before we went back to the dorm room, the doctor told us to stay in the dorm complex and to "please stay out of trouble." This was totally unfair. We did not intentionally look for trouble; it just seemed to find us. We headed back to the dorm building. We had every intention of just relaxing and playing cards and scrabble all weekend long. We really did have good intentions.

Friday night, the weatherman on TV said that the temperature would drop to below freezing. The dorm building did not turn on the heat until the middle of October, and it was still September. Now what would we do? We turned on the oven to 400 degrees and opened the oven door. We wrapped Betty in blankets and put her in a pair of my warm pajamas. I was beginning to think that I was the only one who thought to bring warm clothes. Perhaps living in Wisconsin had prepared me more than my two cream-puff siblings.

We settled down to watch TV and to try to keep warm until morning. Betty was now wrapped up in blankets, propped up in bed, watching TV. We ate salami with cheese and crackers while watching TV. The boys had stocked the refrigerator with diet pop, mineral water, and snack items. We still ate our main meals in the cafeteria, but we did have the option of making soup and sandwiches in the dorm now.

As the night wore on, I become very comfortable, not cold at all. Betty even said that she was too warm. Even Lois felt warm. I turned off the oven; Betty removed all of the blankets she was wrapped up in. Apparently, the campus felt that below freezing constituted a very good reason for turning on the heat early. *Yippee!* Finally, something went right. This was one day when we hadn't had anything go wrong. Is this a good sign? Don't bet on it.

CHAPTER SIXTEEN

✻

THE POWER OF PRAYER

This book would not be complete without mentioning all of the support we received from family and friends. We also received prayers and support from many people we had never met and probably never will meet. We wish to thank everyone who supported us and cared about us. We could not have made it through everything that was happening to us without them.

Of course, we did need to have a good sense of humor, too. Without our sense of humor, we would have gone insane a long time ago. Perhaps we are insane.

As I mentioned earlier, we had a phone in the dorm room, but we were only able to receive calls, not make them. During the evening when we would be watching TV or playing cards, we would receive phone calls from family and friends. All of these calls were to wish us well, to see how we were holding up, and to tell us that everyone was praying for us.

There was a men's morning prayer group which had sent us cards and told us they were continuing to pray for us. There was a women's prayer group also praying for us. There was the whole grade school system in Danville praying for us.

Betty had worked for the school system as a secretary in one of the grade schools before working for the police department. When the children heard what she was going through, they took it upon themselves to hold assemblies and to pray for the both of us. Of course, the poor children had to keep getting together and continue their prayer vigil since surgery kept getting postponed all of the time, but they persisted. Children's voices raised in prayer are the sweetest voices that there are. Young children are innocent and pure of heart; they have yet to grow cynical and prejudicial. God loves to hear the voices of young children. Even Lois's little grandchildren had gotten their grade school classes involved in praying for us.

In fact, one evening, one of the little darlings was upset because she had gone to class to update her teacher and classmates and the poor dear had gotten Betty and me mixed up. The poor child was afraid that perhaps God would get us mixed up in the operating room because she had given the wrong names as to who the donor was and who the recipient was. We assured the distraught child that nothing of the kind would happen and that God knew who was whom. After the phone call, however, we did double our efforts in making those sticky notes with our body parts labeled on them.

Whose idea was it not to allow prayer in school? I have recently been of the opinion that, if they allowed prayer back in the school system, the guns would leave the school system. I know of no one who has ever been hurt or abused because they have been involved in prayer. Some of these modern parents really scare me. No wonder our world is in such a mixed-up state.

I will never understand why a parent would dislike their child being around a prayer. What sort of "bad influence" could a simple prayer cause? What are these parents afraid of? In Eau Claire, we once had a group of people protest the display of a nativity scene in one of our city parks. They were of the opinion that it violated their rights. I figure these people are really very insecure individuals who could really use some prayerful help.

I am not someone who believes that religion should be forced on people. I am not even a big fan of organized religion. I have seen these so-called Christians who are active in their churches and attend faithfully every Sunday go out during the week to their jobs and go about their daily living and treat people terribly. These are the people who, at work, play, and school, gossip about their co-workers, friends, and classmates. Not only do they gossip, but they also spread rumors about them. They don't realize the hurt they cause.

They call themselves Christians? I think not. They are what I call Seventh Day Christians. Organized religion has become a social country club for some people. They feel that, if they attend church on Sunday and are active in church activities that they have earned the right to be called Christians. Somehow I believe they have missed something very important here.

I promise that this is as close as I will get to being preachy in this marvelous literary work of art. Anyway, we had all of these people praying for us; things had to get better. Although perhaps we sisters should change our last name to Murphy. I am sure you have heard of Murphy's law: whatever can go wrong, will. We are now up to Saturday evening, the 23 of September. What could go wrong just had.

CHAPTER SEVENTEEN

THE RED CAR

The hospital in Chicago is situated very close to the downtown area. We could see the Chicago skyline quite clearly on all of our walks to and from the hospital and doctor's office. The skyline is really impressive, especially at night, but you certainly do not want to be out on the streets admiring it. The campus is just three blocks away from Little Italy, three blocks away from murder and mayhem. To offset this environmental hazard, the university offers a service called the Red Car.

This is a bright red van with a flashing yellow light on top of it which operates during the hours when all of the crazies come out to play. The Red Car operates from six p.m. to twelve p.m. and from five a.m. to seven a.m. This service is to ensure that you don't get mugged, murdered, or raped while on campus. If you need to be out at any hours other than the ones during which the Red Car operates, you're on your own. We did have a can of pepper spray that the officers had given Betty for protection. Something tells me that the officers in Danville were quite aware of what Chicago is like.

On Saturday evening, September 23, Betty and I were just settling down to watch the new series *JAG* on TV. Betty decided to put one of the new solution bags into her portable warmer to warm the solution to body temperature. There is nothing worse than pouring cold solution into a body with a temperature of 98.6 degrees.

While getting the bag out for her, I noticed that the bag did not look exactly like the ones she had brought from home. There was no tubing attached to it. It looked just like a normal bag of saline solution that they use in hospitals for IVs. I showed the bag to Betty. The solution in the bag was the correct solution, but the kind of bag they had it in is not the type of bag she had to have to hook up to the tubing she had coming out of her abdomen. Oh, no! We have big problems here.

Betty was unable to do her last dialysis for the evening; she could not hook up the new bags to her dialysis tubing. Now what were we to do? Lois and Betty went downstairs to the lobby to call the transplant unit at the hospital. When they came back up to the dorm room, it was to await a return call from Stormin' Norman.

A half hour later, the phone rang. Stormin' Norman was out of town for a few days. *Great!* The hospital had located Pat, the lady from whom we got the dorm room key. Pat headed up the liver transplant part of the transplant unit; Stormin' Norman handled the kidney section. Pat told us to get Betty up to the hospital and up to the seventh floor to the transplant unit so that they could try to figure something out. Betty and Lois bundled up and headed to the lobby to call the Red Car to take them to the hospital. I stayed at the dorm.

At the hospital, they had no tubing that would fit the tubing in Betty's abdomen. The nurse called Anne from the pharmacy, who brought up all the tubing she had. No go! They had no tubing that would fit. They sat around and scratched their heads for a while, trying to figure this new problem out.

Finally, they called in a nurse from another floor whose name was Molly. Molly used to work in the kidney transplant unit, and they thought she might have some clue as to what to do. After many trials and errors (and many hours of waiting), Molly was finally able to rig up a temporary tubing apparatus that would work. She then showed Betty how to do the dialysis and went through a complete dialysis with her.

Meanwhile, the rest of the staff on the transplant floor were scurrying around like mad. A liver had just arrived (in a cooler no less), and a young man, who was hemorrhaging badly, was brought in for an immediate transplant. Of course, Betty and Lois had to peak into the ice chest to see the liver. They left the hospital just as the surgical team wheeled the young man into surgery.

It was now after midnight, and the Red Car did not run anymore. How were the two city slickers going to make it back to the dorm? Thoughts of murder, rape, and gun shots raced through their scared heads. One of the nurses on the floor called the Red Car and explained that they needed them to transport Betty and Lois back to the dorm as it was a medical emergency. She had to resort to cussing and finally to threats before she was able to get the Red Car to come get the girls. They arrived at the dorm at one a.m.

We decided that we needed a good night's sleep and that, since tomorrow was Sunday, we would all spend a nice, quite, restful, and peaceful day relaxing. After all, Sunday is supposed to be a day of rest, right? *Wrong!*

CHAPTER EIGHTEEN

✯

FIRE!

Sunday, September 24, 1995, dawned bright and sunny. Lois's husband, Vince, and her daughter, Carey, were arriving on the Amtrak at about twelve-thirty to visit for the day.

The dorm room had an intercom system that allowed someone from the lobby to buzz the room. You were then able to talk to them and push a button that would allow the outside building door to open to let them in.

Lois discovered this little device when my son Bill, back on Monday, pushed the button in the downstairs lobby so that we would unlock the door so he could come up to the room. She had no idea where the buzzing sound was coming from. She finally discovered that it was from the little box next to the door.

She pushed the button and said, "Hello? Who's there?"

Bill said, "It's Bill."

Lois said, "Bill who?"

I cannot for the life of me figure out how she could forget who her own nephew was, but she did. She did finally let the poor kid into the building.

I awoke at about eight a.m. on Sunday and took a shower. Lois and Betty were still sleeping. I was out of the shower and dressed, getting ready to dry my hair when a very *loud* continuous alarm goes off. I opened the bathroom door to find Lois at the intercom. "Hello? Helloooooo?"

I couldn't believe this woman! "It's the fire alarm!" I shouted above all the noise.

Betty and Lois were in their pajamas; I was dressed but had a wet head. I stuck my head out into the hallway and saw three firemen coming down the hallway towards me. I began to think that we are all going to die. How in the heck were we going to get Betty down to the street level? We couldn't take the elevator; we certainly couldn't get the wheelchair down the stairway. Should we just push her down the stairs and hope for the best?

All of these questions were going through my mind as I watched the firemen run down the hallway towards me. They stopped at the apartment door next to ours and knocked.

"Are you cooking again?" they shouted.

Some foreign students opened the door, smiled, and giggled; they answer yes. Ten minutes later, the alarm finally quit.

About one p.m., Lois went over to "Chicago Hopeless" to attend chapel. After all of the excitement, I decided I needed some fresh air. We were not supposed to leave the dorm, but I figured that the street seemed safer at this point than the building did. I went for a walk.

As I came back from my walk and entered the building, the fire alarms went off again. All of the fire doors in the building slammed shut. Betty was alone on the second floor. I was in the lobby closed off by the fire doors. I quickly pushed the elevator button. I knew that this was the wrong thing to do, but I had to try to reach my sister before the fire did. I raced into the dorm room to find Betty calmly watching TV. You could not hear the alarm up there.

"What's the rush?" she asks.

I told her to look out the window. Again, we had three hook and ladder trucks surrounding the front of the building. Looking out of the window, we saw Lois streaking down the street, heading for the front of the building. The firemen won't let her through. Betty and I looked at each other.

"Do you think someone is cooking again?" I asked.

"Must be," Betty replied. We calmly sat down and watched TV. Ten minutes later, a breathless Lois arrived in the room.

"How was church?" we ask her.

"Did you guys hear the fire alarms?" Lois squeaked.

We told her one of the students from Pakistan burned his lunch. Apparently, this is a regular occurrence in this building. These soon-to-be doctors are not very good cooks. The students set the fire alarm off on a regular basis. These students are going to be the future doctors of the world. Kind of scary, isn't it?

Vince and Carey arrived, and Lois took them on a tour of the campus. Betty and I took the scrabble game outside to the courtyard to sit in the sun and relax. We were sitting there when I noticed a horrible smell.

"Do you smell that?" I asked.

Betty said that it smelled like something had died. I looked over a few feet from where we are sitting and saw water bubbling up from the ground. The sewer had backed up. We decided that perhaps we should go back inside. Even though the building was a potential fire trap, it was probably safer than sitting by a toxic waste dump.

Well, so much for a quiet, restful, and peaceful weekend. Again, we did not go looking for any trouble; it just seemed to find us. Is it just something about us? Are we the modern day version of Job? Is it this city? What else could go wrong? Don't ask!

CHAPTER NINETEEN

※

BACK TO "CHICAGO HOPELESS"

Monday, September 25, arrived, the day we were finally going to check into the hospital. We were to be at the hospital at eleven a.m. During the morning, every time the phone rang we would cringe, wondering if it would be the doctor's office telling us that surgery had to be canceled. We had learned from Stormin' Norman that only one out of four transplants actually goes through. The patients will make it to Chicago, but something happens, and surgery is called off at the last minute. We were a bundle of nerves.

At ten-thirty, we loaded Betty into the wheelchair along with overnight cases and a plastic bag with her solution hanging on the IV holder. I walked alongside them, carrying my overnight case and various plastic bags. We looked exactly like three bag ladies. We got some curious stares as we traversed the sidewalks on our way to the hospital. We were finally on our way to being admitted to the seventh floor transplant unit of "Chicago Hopeless."

There is something I should explain here. English does not seem to be the main language spoken at "Chicago Hopeless." The hospital is situated in a major city in the middle of the United States of America, but English is a secondary language here. Spanish is the primary language, along with some sort of street jive. This street jive kind of reminds you of chickens in a farm yard. There is a lot of hand movement, and the head seems to move from side to side while the people are conversing with one another. It really is a strange sight. They seem to be speaking English, but you can't understand what they are saying. You really feel like a foreigner here. It is very hard to be understood. Getting admitted was not an easy thing to do; we had the language barrier with which to contend, for one thing.

Upon arriving at the hospital, we left the wheelchair in the lobby to be found by the owners. Upon arriving on the seventh floor, the nurse immediately took me into my room to take my temperature. It was normal. I sighed in relief. She was about to take by blood pressure, and I explained to her that it would probably be high but that it was nothing to worry about, just nerves. She looked at me strangely and told me that my blood pressure was perfectly normal. Not only was my blood pressure fine, but so were my heart rate and my urine tests. Hooray! Surgery was a definite go!

The seventh floor transplant unit had the nurses' station situated in the center of the floor with the patients' rooms in a square around the nurses' station. The donor was put in a room on one side of the nurses' station, and the recipient was put in a room on the opposite side of the floor. The reason for this was to encourage patients to walk back and forth to each other's rooms after surgery to visit. They deliberately put patients a great deal of distance apart so that they had to walk. They want patients to exercise after surgery. This did not seem so bad when they explained it to us, but, after surgery, I considered it cruel and unusual punishment. Also, the recipients needed to be in rooms with special monitors in them, and the donors did not. This donor did need to be in a room with monitors, but we will get into that in a later chapter.

The man for the TV came into my room. He asked me if I would like the TV turned on. I told him that it was Monday and that *Chicago*

Hope was on later, so of course I wanted the TV turned on. He told me it would cost $4.00 a day. I did not bring my purse, so I told him to find Lois, and she would pay for it. I also told him that my sister, Betty, would want her TV on, also. He turned my TV on, showed me how to operate the remote, and then went to turn Betty's TV on.

Betty's TV would not operate with the remote. Her outlet was not working, so the TV had to be turned on and off manually. He gave me back the $4.00 for Betty's TV. He decided that he would not charge her for a TV that did not work properly. Now I was the designated channel-turner and the one Betty called to turn the TV on and off for her.

I told the man that our surgery was the next day and that neither one of us would want to pay for any TV. He said it was no problem. They came by every day and collected money for the TV, so tomorrow they just would not come by. It eventually turned out that Betty received free TV for the whole visit. I was still the official person who turned the dang thing on and off and changed the channels. This did become an actual *pain* after we had surgery.

Lois headed back to the dorm room at five p.m. She would return at six a.m. tomorrow to be with me before I went down for surgery. I was scheduled for surgery at seven a.m.; Betty was scheduled for one p.m.

Betty decided to come to my room to watch *Chicago Hope*. She came in after dinner, and we both got into my bed to watch TV. This did look a bit strange; the hospital bed was a single bed, so it was a bit cramped. We did get some snickers from the nursing staff passing by.

Betty's three boys arrived after dinner and visited with us until visiting hours were over. They were allowed in the unit that night and all day the next day. After that, visiting times and the length of the visit would be severely curtailed. Betty and I settled down for a good night's sleep; we were ready for the next day. The day of surgery was finally here.

CHAPTER TWENTY

TWO WRIGHTS CAN MAKE A WRONG

I should mention here that we discovered that there was another patient on the transplant unit with the last name of Wright. This lady's first name, however, was Mary. Her room was right next door to Betty's, and her son's room (he had donated a kidney to her the week before) was right next door to my room. This mother and son also came from Danville, Illinois. The doctor we had was also the surgeon who performed their transplant. Talk about coincidence.

After we watched *Chicago Hope*, I walked with Betty back to her room. On the way, we met the doctor who was coming in to see us. He told Betty that there was a lady in the room next door to hers that he wanted her to meet. He said the patient's name was Betty Wright, that she came from Danville, and that he had done a kidney transplant on her the week before.

Betty and I looked at each other. I walked over to the doctor, and I placed my arm around his shoulders. "Hey, doc," I said, pointing to Betty, "this is Betty Wright." I then pointed to myself. "I'm Shirley, her sister. I am the kidney donor; Betty is the kidney recipient. You are operating on us tomorrow; you will take my right kidney and give it to Betty. Do we have this straight? Should we perhaps put the Post-it notes on now?" He just smiled and said that he had the first names mixed up. We told him that we hoped that was all he was going to get mixed up.

How he could get the two mixed up totally confused us. All people are created equal. I agree with that statement. Some people are born with white skin, some with black, yellow, red skin. Now, the Mrs. Wright that was next door to Betty was an African American; Betty is Caucasian. You can now understand why we became confused and a little worried. He not only got the names mixed up but was color blind to boot!

CHAPTER TWENTY-ONE

✻

RISE AND SHINE!

We have now arrived, at this point in this narrative, at the night before surgery. My sister had left and gone to her room. I was now alone. A male nurse came in, asking me if I would like something to help me to sleep. I, of course, willingly took him up on the offer since my mind was traveling at the speed of light, and sleep was many light-years away. He returned to give me the pill.

"Here is your Benadryl," he said.

"I don't have hives; I'm not having an allergic reaction to anything. Why do I want to take an antihistamine?" was my response.

"We give this out as a sleeping pill," he answered. "It makes people drowsy."

"Drowsy, to me, means close to, but not quite, asleep" was my reply.

"Do you want it or not?" was his cryptic response.

"Sure, at this point, I'll take anything." I replied.

He gave me the pill; I swallowed it and was wide awake until two in the morning. I finally drifted off to something close to sleep but not quite there. At three-thirty, my light came on.

"It's time to get up and get ready!" boomed the voice of a large (I use that term loosely) female nurse. She gave me a towel and washcloth and told me to go into the bathroom and wash up. I could brush my teeth, but I couldn't swallow any of the water if I rinsed my mouth. She left.

I did as she requested, then sat on the edge of my bed, waiting for her to return. At four, another nurse came in, wanting to know why I was still up and awake.

Now I was confused.

"A nurse came in a half an hour ago and told me to get up and washed up," I said.

"Well," she replied, "it's too early for you to be up. Go back to sleep." She promptly turned off the light and left.

Now, there was no way in h…no way that I was going to get back to sleep.

At five-thirty, my sister, Lois, arrived with a real good-looking guy in surgical scrubs. I hadn't seen one living soul since Attila the Nurse shut the lights off. The man with my sister was the anesthesiologist.

"I'll be back in a short while to give you a shot to relax you. Then we will wheel you down to surgery at six-thirty. You'll be too groggy to know what is going on, totally relaxed," he told me.

"I like relaxed. Couldn't you just put me under before we even wheel down to surgery?" was my squeaky reply.

He laughed and exited. At six, I was wondering where the cute guy in the scrubs disappeared to. At six-fifteen, I was panicking. When they came in at six-thirty, they had to pry my hands off of the bed rails to get me onto the gurney.

"It's a mistake," I yelled. "I'm not relaxed yet; he was supposed to come back to give me a shot. You can't take me; I haven't had the shot yet," I screamed.

No one listened. I was dragged, kicking and screaming, down to the surgical floor. My sister was trying to reassure me. It wasn't working. I was laying on a gurney in the hallway when another nurse with all sorts of scrubs, masks, head gear, and what not appears beside me.

"You don't look the least bit sleepy to me," she says. "Usually, by the time I see the patients, they are totally out of it."

"I'm just totally out of my mind right now," I responded. "I haven't had my shot yet."

"Well," she replied, "they are ready for you, and here we go."

She then proceeded to push me into a room. I was yelling and screaming at this point. Finally, the cute guy returned.

"Gee, I wasn't able to get back to you. How are you doing?"

Was this guy nuts or just plain stupid?

"Where's my shot?" I yelled.

"Hey, patients never get to see the inside of the surgical room, and you'll be the first."

"Pardon me for not being more excited about the prospect, but I want to be *put out, NOW!*"

"Relax," he replied, "I'll give you a shot just as soon as we get you on the table."

"You'll have to get me on the table first, and, if I'm awake, the odds are not good that you'll accomplish that feat," I said.

He laughed and told me to get on the table.

"What table?" I asked.

"This one," he replied, pointing to what looked like a crucifixion cross.

"Oh, no," I said, and decided to leave the room.

Three of them got me onto the table and strapped me down. I got my shot; a big one. Then the doctor came in. He was real fuzzy, and I couldn't quite make out what he was saying to me. His words seemed to have an echo to them. Something was put on my face, and…

My next conscious thought was that someone was calling my name. I opened my eyes and saw my nephew, Brad, bending over me. I thought that I'd died and gone to hell. Why was he in there? I soon found out.

A nurse came over. "You're not supposed to be in here," she said to Brad.

My nephew is not a small person; he sort of goes where he wants to when he wants to.

"I'm checking on my aunt. No one was telling us anything, and it has been over eight hours since she went to surgery. A surgery procedure, we were told, that was supposed to take four hours," said my nephew.

I don't know what happened after that. I hurt, I was sleepy (finally), and now people were poking and prodding me and calling my name all the time.

"Do you know who you are?" a male nurse asked me.

"Why?" I replied. "Don't you know who I am? I'm not a bit surprised with the way things are run around this hospital. You have cockroaches roaming the hallways, did you know that?"

"I need you to tell me who you are," a calm voice replied.

I didn't reply.

"Do you know where you are?" I heard the sound of the calm voice and then felt a shaking sensation as he gently shook my shoulder.

"Hell," I responded. "I've died and gone to hell."

"What is your name?" the voice asked again.

"Go away. I hurt, and I want to sleep," I answered.

"Not until you tell me your name," the voice replied.

"I want a lawyer. You people obviously are not qualified to run a hospital, let alone do major surgery on people. You don't know who I am, yet you just operated on me," I replied.

My nephew finally told them that, in this mood, I probably wouldn't tell them who I was and that, if I could argue with them, I was just fine.

Now the room started to spin; the bed was moving. My side hurt, my stomach hurt, and my back hurt. The ride down the hall was bumpy, probably from running over the cockroaches. I thought I could hear them crunching as the bed rolled.

They wanted me to move into another bed. I liked the one I was in just fine. I was picked up; it hurt. My stomach felt like it was going to erupt. My head was spinning. People kept looking at me and asking questions I can't answer. I wanted them to leave me alone. They wanted me to breathe into some stupid plastic thing. They yelled at me. It hurt to breathe into it; I wouldn't do it.

Night and day were the same to me. I hurt badly. I saw people leaning over me. Someone told me to push the button I was holding. I finally registered the meaning: push button, pain medicine comes. I pushed, and I pushed, and I pushed.

I slept; they woke me up. They rolled me over, pounded on my back. "You have a fever," they shout, "you must clear your lungs. Cough!" It hurt to cough, it hurt to breathe. They pounded on my back and kept coming in to pound on my back.

I was finally awake. I really hurt. I was thirsty. I pushed the call button.

An hour later, someone came in. At least it seemed like an hour later. I asked for a drink of water. They wouldn't let me have any water to drink. My lips were dried and cracked. I fell back to sleep.

My sister Lois came in.

"How are you, sweetie?" she asked.

"I'm thirsty," I replied.

"I'll see if I can get you some water," she says, and leaves.

When she came back, it was to tell me that I couldn't have anything to drink. I asked what time it was. I found out that it was two days after surgery. No wonder I was thirsty. I begged all day for water and couldn't have any.

Finally, a little nurse (another foreigner) gave me a piece of gauze that she had gotten wet. This was just to wipe over my lips. She left me with the little piece of gauze. I sucked it dry. I kept asking for little pieces of gauze whenever I could, and then I would suck them totally dry. Then Attila the Nurse came back on duty. The little pieces of gauze now came to me just barely damp; I couldn't suck even a drop out of it. I was getting desperate, I wanted water so badly.

On the third day, they let me sit up to brush my teeth. I was thinking, brush teeth, water in glass to rinse teeth, *yes!* Sure enough, I get the toothbrush, toothpaste, bowl, and a *glass of water.* Oh, heavenly day! Before I could get the glass to my mouth, Attila the Nurse arrived and snatched it away from me.

"Oh, no, you don't. No water means *no water!*"

She left. I noticed a small bottle of mouthwash, and I drank the whole thing. When she came back into the room, she noticed that I have the freshest breath in all of Chicago, so fresh, in fact, that it could knock you over with the minty fresh smell of it. She gave me a very dirty look. I smiled at her and thought *bitch*.

CHAPTER TWENTY-TWO

"HELP! I CAN'T BREATHE!"

My victory with the mouthwash was very short-lived. I was sitting, dangling my feel over the side of the bed, tied to tubes and whatnot, and I was finding it difficult to breathe. I hit the call light. I was getting light-headed, and I was afraid I was dying and still unable to breathe. No one came.

I was nearly unconscious when one of the specialist's "almost doctors" walked by my room. Seeing that I was gasping for air, he sprang into action. There is no other word for it; "sprang" defines it. One minute he was in the hall; the next, he was up in the air, then he landed beside my bed. Sort of like a rendition of Batman.

Lights, bells, whistles, intercom systems were all activated at once. Apparently, there is a special button that was in the room. When it is pressed the whole hospital staff appears in your room all at once. At least that was what it seemed like.

An oxygen mask was put on my face; my bed was lowered. I was thinking that I was at a convention of "almost doctors," the star attraction, no less. I couldn't breathe with the bed lowered. I couldn't get them to understand me with that contraption over my mouth. I tried to remove it; they pushed it back. Everyone was yelling at the same time.

I finally got the strength to punch one of the "almost doctors," and he fell to the floor. I whipped off the mask before anyone could grab it. "*I need to sit up!*" I screamed. I wasn't stupid; I immediately put the mask back on because it meant *air*. They finally understood what I was trying to convey to them. The bed was raised up.

They thought I was bleeding internally. Bed and all, I was pushed to the elevators and whisked down to who knows where. I was given an ultrasound. Then I was whisked right back up to my room. My heartbeat was at 120. Now, this isn't something that concerned me because I had no idea what it was supposed to be.

I was hooked up to machines to monitor my heart. If my heart rate went up over the 120, alarms went off. I couldn't move a muscle, or I set the thing off, and the whole hospital would, again, be in my room. I'd never had so much attention in my life.

Day four wasn't any better. I was still hooked up to machines, oxygen, the pain medicine machine, and IV tubes. I had something plugged into every opening in my body. I still couldn't have any water. My first priority was *water*. Every time I moved, the alarms went off. I was getting tired of it all.

Attila the Nurse came in. Tests had been ordered; someone would be coming for me. From the way she put it, I was expecting the grim raper" to appear in my doorway at any minute.

This kid arrived. I am not being prejudiced here but, the kid spoke some kind of street language that I needed an interpreter just to understand. Apparently, I was to "get on the gurney." Attila the Nurse finally translated for me. I did manage to point out that the gurney did not have any sheet, blanket, pillow, or anything. However, I was surprised that it did have wheels.

"I ain't got no urders on dis here form that says nutin' 'bout no shits [I am quoting here, and I swear this is the way he pronounced it], pillers, or nutin' else. Dis here liddy has ta git her ass on dat dere table, and we'uns has gotta roll! Now, is ya or is ya ain't gittin yur butt on dat roller, boy!" This is what he said; I swear!

I got my butt onto the roller thingy with my open gown flapping in the breeze. We rolled on down to the testing place, which is by the morgue. I was really getting concerned here. Besides, it was *da*...it was cold in the hallway. I had no blanket, no sheet, my gown was open in the back, and I was left in a deserted hallway in the basement of the hospital.

I kept calling out. I still couldn't get up to walk. My pain medicine box was left upstairs. I had a "live" oxygen tank laying on the gurney next to me, and they didn't even hand me a "No Smoking" sign to carry along. Finally, some nurse came along.

"I'm really not dead!" I pleaded.

"Well," she said, "of course your not. What are you doing down here?"

"I wish I knew." I was sobbing by now. "Some guy who doesn't speak English, even though he is American, left me here. I am supposed to have tests."

"Not here you won't; this is the basement," she said. "If you're not dead, you don't belong down here."

She took me upstairs, gave me a sheet to cover my shivering body, and left me again to my own devices. I was so exhausted that I fell asleep. Someone finally came along and wheeled me in for another test. This technician asked when I'd had surgery. I told her that it had been four days ago.

She noticed that my lips were very cracked. I told her I was thirsty. She brought me a glass of water. She was an angel. She had a halo around her head. She showed up as a bright golden light before my eyes. I drank my fill of water, my first drink in four days. That is, of course, not counting the mouthwash.

When she was done with the test, I asked her if I could have some more water. I, again, drank my fill. I figured that I'd better store it up before I got back to Attila the Nurse.

Tests revealed that I didn't have any bleeding. They couldn't find anything except that my blood gases were low. All of this was probably due to lack of water, I figured. I was removed from the critical list since I was breathing. I did have the near-miss with the morgue, but, luckily, the observant nurse did notice that, if I was talking, I couldn't be dead. I was thankful for that.

Back in my room, the machines were hooked back up. I was covered with blankets because I was shivering so hard after my trip around the hospital. Every time I moved, the heart machine would go off. I finally got tired of it and took all the electrodes off. Over the PA, I heard "*Code Blue!*" and my room number. Again, the whole hospital was in my room.

I said "hi" and sort of smiled at them all standing there in the doorway looking at me.

The electrodes were reattached, and I was threatened with bodily harm if I tried to remove them again.

CHAPTER TWENTY-THREE

✵

"WATER! PLEASE? I NEED WATER!"

Now, I was still weak and in a lot of pain. A couple of hours after the "Code Blue" episode, I was able to convince one of the "almost doctors" to take the machines off of me. Since they couldn't figure out what was wrong and since I was talking and breathing, they agreed. It was now time for me to get up and walk a bit.

My sister Lois had left that morning for Europe. I was off the critical list, and their vacation had been planned for months. The surgery had been postponed so many times that we were months late having it done. She flew the coup.

There was a bit of information that no one had given me. My sister, Betty, the recipient of my kidney, had "died" on the operating table but had been "revived." She had been in critical condition for three days. Keep in mind, my sister was in the room where the nurse call button did not work, the TV remote didn't work, and all sorts of other odds and ends were broken. Great hospital, huh?

The two "almost doctors" came in to get me up and take me for a walk to see my sister. They told me what had happened. I was furious that I hadn't known about it. With my two "book-end" doctors, I slowly walked, pushing my IV pole along with us, to my sister's room. She was sitting up in bed, eating, drinking, and having a great time watching TV.

I was furious. "How dare you almost die after all I went through to give you that ***** kidney?"

She laughed at me. She told me she was glad I was finally up and around. She had been in to see me the day before, but I had been totally out of it. I had given everyone a scare; they thought they were losing me.

I hobbled back to my room with my two "book-end" doctors.

Attila the Nurse came in. I again asked for water.

"You can't have water until the doctor indicates it on his chart," she explained. "Your chart still says 'nothing by mouth.' You have an IV; you're getting plenty of fluids. Besides, if you drink water too soon, you will swell up and burst all of your stitches out."

"Could I take that chance?" I pleaded.

She just huffed and left the room. One of the "almost doctors" was still in the room. He felt very sorry for me.

"I don't understand the doctor on this," he said. "I'll get you some ice chips, but you have to promise you won't tell *anyone!*"

I promised and offered to sign it in blood. He looked at me real strange....Perhaps I should explain something that I totally forgot to mention. Maybe it was because the days seemed to just blend into each other at this point. Perhaps it was the morphine drip that I was attached to.

Anyway, on day three after the surgery, when all of the tests were taken and I had been placed on the critical list, it was noted that my blood count was very low. I spent day three in bed getting IV's of blood. I mean, it was *all day*. That is one of the reasons that I hadn't been up out of bed; I still had a catheter and was still hooked up to my pain machine.

Once I received all of this blood, my heart rate seemed to go back to normal. They never did decide if I had been bleeding internally.

Perhaps, if I had been, my body fixed it all by itself. At least my body knew what to do; none of the doctors seemed capable of figuring anything out.

So mentioning signing anything in blood after what we had all been through with me was not a smart thing to say. He did bring me a cup of ice chips, stood outside my room, and kept an eye out for Attila the Nurse while I chomped them down. He then took the cup back and left to destroy the evidence. I felt much better.

Now that I was mobile, I was able to visit Betty on a regular basis. Someone had to watch out for her. She had no call button, the TV remote didn't work, and she tends to get bored and lonely very quickly. Now, my incision was from the middle of my stomach to the middle of my back going around my body in a half-circle. Betty had a four-inch incision just under her belly button.

Somehow I felt that I had received the short end of the stick here. She got all of the attention of the staff; all she had to do was sigh, and they came running to her. She got all the diet Pepsi she wanted, great food, and people checking on her. I was totally ignored—unless I was inadvertently setting off alarms, that is—and never saw a "real" doctor the rest of the time that I was in the hospital. It was as if, once I had given the body part, they had forgotten I existed. I was hungry, I was thirsty, and it had been four days since I had eaten or had a drink of anything. Well, except for snitching drinks of water and mouthwash whenever I could.

I would go into Betty's room, and she would have a snack, a big meal, a can of Pepsi, a sandwich, or a glass of juice. I hated going in to visit her. I should also explain something here. Once Betty recovered from her "near death" experience, she bounced right back. The first morning after her surgery, she immediately had a bowel movement and was given liquids and started on foods.

I finally asked Attila the Nurse when I would be allowed to eat and drink.

"Not till you have a bowel movement," she said.

Let's figure something out here. I hadn't had anything to eat in over four days. How was I to have a bowel movement? I mentioned this to her.

"Let me get this straight. In order for you to feed me, I have to shit. Before I can shit, don't I have to have something in my system to create the shit? Since I haven't had anything in over four days, how was I to create this shit?"

She looked puzzled for a moment. She said she would leave a message for the doctor. I think I actually stumped the woman.

Later that day, my "almost doctor" friend came in to check on me. He explained that the doctor had forgotten to write on my chart that I could have liquids after forty-eight hours and that I should have been on solids for the last two days.

By this time, I was so used to the treatment I had been receiving that I wasn't a bit surprised that the hospital and doctor had just forgotten all about me. He immediately got me some water, and he ordered a tray of broth and Jell-O to start me off. Here I was, at ten at night on the fourth day after surgery, finally eating and drinking something.

At this point, I was unhooked from all of my machinery except the IV bag, and I was dragging that around with me as I traversed back and forth between my room and my sister's. I was no longer receiving pain medication via a pain machine, but I was told to ask for pain medication when I was uncomfortable. Now, with all of this added activity, I was reaching up to change the channels on my sister's TV, running to the nurses' station to get a nurse because her call light doesn't work, and sneaking out of the transplant unit to get a diet Coke from the downstairs vending machine.

I should explain here that, since they had refused me liquids for so long, once I became mobile, I would sneak out of the transplant unit (not easy to do in a hospital gown dragging an IV cart along), go down the elevator to the main floor and to the soda machine. I would really get people starring at me. Then, I would sneak back up and into my room.

I got pretty good at it. I would smuggle snacks up to Betty from the vending machines. I even went through the line in the hospital cafeteria, and no one questioned me. Chicago is really strange that way. Besides, after surgery, I was trying to prove that I really was invisible. Nobody seemed to care one way or the other about me.

Now the race was on to have a bowel movement. I was getting trays of real food. At least that is what they called it. It was horrible! Attila the Nurse used to tell me I had to clean the tray. It was so bad that I would wait till she was gone, hobble into the bathroom, and flush it down the toilet.

Once everyone was settled into doing their "hospital things," I would sneak down to the cafeteria and have a real meal. I was getting up the nerve to leave the hospital and head to Kentucky Fried Chicken, but I was caught at the door and escorted back to the unit. That ended my forays for a bit.

On the Saturday after surgery (surgery had been on Tuesday), my "almost doctor" friend told me that I could leave the hospital and be discharged on Sunday. Of course, I had to have a bowel movement before that could happen. I was now convinced that I would be safer alone at the dorm, taking care of myself, than in "Chicago Hopeless," waiting to be killed by the so-called medical professionals.

It hurt to try to go to the bathroom. Having an incision that large was going to cause me a problem in this area. I was determined to leave this den of torture. I snuck down to the cafeteria to make sure I could eat a decent meal and prayed for a bowel movement.

On my last day in the hospital, I was unhooked from my IV. All of the walking around I was doing and climbing chairs to turn the channels on Betty's TV was causing me a lot of pain. I pushed my call button. No one came. Why was I not surprised about this?

After an hour, the pain was really bad. I hurt, really hurt. I hobbled to the front desk. My posture at this time seemed to be permanently stooped over so as to not pull on my incision. I had yet to see the damage that they had done to me. I tried but couldn't see in the tiny mirror in my bathroom. I was almost to the front desk when one of the male nurses came up to me.

"I need a pain pill," I gasped.

"I'll get you a Tylenol," he replied.

That did it! I found some inner strength, grabbed the front of his uniform shirt, dragged him down to my eye level, and said (excuse my language here, but I was pissed!), "I have been sliced open from my belly button to the middle of my back. I don't have a fucking headache; I said that *I am in pain!*"

He immediately checked my chart. They had been giving me regular Tylenol, and the doctor had ordered pain medication. For the last two days, I had been in agony, taking what I thought was something for pain and only getting relief for a headache I didn't have. I was given my pain pills on a regular basis after that.

Now I was totally convinced that they were trying to kill me. I strained even harder for that bowel movement.

CHAPTER TWENTY-FOUR

✹

EUREKA!

Saturday evening I passed some gas. I figured that was close enough. When my "almost doctor" friend came in that evening, I asked about my discharge. I received the usual spiel about the bowel movement. I will admit here that I was in fear of my life. I lied.

"But I had one," I innocently said.

"Did you save it?" he asked.

"Was I supposed to?" I asked. "I don't usually do that. I didn't know the hospital collected such things, or is it just a personal fetish of yours?"

He looked at me; I think he knew I wasn't being totally honest. "I'll mark it on your chart that you did, but, if you have any problems when you get back to that dorm, you come back here immediately!" he said to me.

I hugged him. I was finally leaving this nightmare of a place! I was ecstatic! He was signing me out the next day. He would look in on me in the morning, and then I could leave. Since I was going to the dorm, he figured I would be okay. He also thought that my sister Lois was still in town and at the dorm. I didn't point out the error of this; I just omitted that little detail. I knew I was going to be safer on my own than in this place.

I had a good night's sleep for the first time in weeks. I told Betty my good news. She still couldn't leave until Tuesday or Wednesday the following week, and that was only to the dorm room with someone there with her. She had to stay in Chicago for a couple of weeks after she was released. Her son Jeff would be coming to stay with her at that time.

On Sunday morning, I got up and dressed in regular clothes. I packed my suitcase, put my hospital stuff in a plastic bag, got my jacket out, and was waiting with baited breathe to be released.

At one, I was finally given the okay to leave. I would have to call the doctor's office on Monday morning to set up an appointment. I could handle that. Someone would come in and take me to the dorm. I waited and, about a half hour later, a little Asian girl came in.

"You go home?" she asked.

"*Yes!*" I enthusiastically replied.

She said, "Okay, you follow me. You have things to take with you?"

I pointed to the potted plant on my tray table, my suitcase and bag on the bed, and my jacket. She picked up the potted plant, turned, and walked out of the room. Now, I had heard that patients usually leave in wheelchairs from hospitals. I had actually seen this in practice, considering I was a professional hospital visitor. No wheelchair.

I picked up my jacket and put it over my arm, picked up my suitcase, then picked up the plastic bag. My arms were full. I limped out after her. She headed to the elevators with me dragging along behind her. I figured that it was a cheap hospital; maybe someone else was stealing wheelchairs now. I guess I considered this my "just desserts" for stealing one for Betty. Once we got outside the hospital, she stopped. I thought we were waiting for a ride. The dorm was a good *long* three blocks away. I hurt.

She said, "What dorm you stay at?"

I told her I was in the residence dorm.

"Long way," she replied, and headed off toward the dorm.

I couldn't believe this. Here I was, looking and walking like Quasimodo from the *Hunchback of Notre Dame*, with no ride and no wheelchair, carrying everything except the small potted plant which she carried. I followed her. It took a while. I had to stop to put things down and sit on retaining walls along the way. I was beginning to see stars in front of my eyes, and I was near to collapsing.

When we finally reached the entrance to the dorm, she turned, handed me the plant (which I had to hold under my chin), and said, "Have a nice day." She walked away.

Now my hands were completely full, my keys were in my pocket, and I had no free hands. My dorm room was on the second floor, and there were two doors to unlock to get into the lobby. I staggered over to a flower bed with raised walls and lowered my body the best I could to rest the plant on the planter. It was a nice plant that had been sent to me in the hospital, but right now I was cursing it.

I finally put everything down and went over and unlocked the door. Then I remembered that you can't unlock the door and shut it because it automatically locks again. My things were ten feet away. I shut the door, went over and picked up the suitcase, and came back to unlock the door again. I got into the first entryway, put the suitcase in the lobby, and repeated the process three more times. Now everything was in the lobby. All I had to do now was get everything up to the second floor. There wasn't a resident in sight.

I piled everything up next to one of the elevators and pushed the button. Naturally, the elevator farthest from me opened. I couldn't possibly move quickly enough, so I let it go. Once the door closed, I waited a couple of minutes and pushed the button again. The same elevator door opened. Okay, I figured, I will move everything over to that elevator. I did this and again pushed the button. The door of the elevator where I had first put my things opened. Now I was ready to cry.

A resident came in. He was either Pakistani or Indian. I asked him if he could help me. He looked at me very strangely. I asked him if he spoke English. He said that he, of course, spoke English. I needed to get my things upstairs to the second floor. He again looked at me funny.

"I just had a kidney removed; I hurt; I need to get my things up to my room in the liver transplant dorm," I pleaded.

"If you had a kidney removed, why you stay in a liver transplant dorm room?" he questioned.

"It's a long story, and you will have grandchildren by the time I could finish explaining it to you," I sighed.

He helped put my things in the elevator, and he pushed the button to go up. He apparently pushed the button for the fourth floor, and I told him I needed to go to the second floor. He said he lived on the fourth floor, and all I needed to do was push the button for the second floor. Aren't people in Chicago nice? I pushed the button, but the elevator had already passed the second floor and was stopping on the fourth floor. He got out and left me.

I pushed the button for the second floor, and, when it finally stopped on the second floor, I pushed the door hold button and picked up my suitcase and carried it out to the hall. Before I could put it down and turn around I heard the elevator door close. I tried pushing the buttons but it had headed upstairs. The rest of my things were on that elevator. God, how I hate this town!

I waited and pushed the button, and the other elevator opened. Now I was playing musical elevators again. I figured I would never see my things again. I was ready to take my suitcase to the dorm room and then come back when the correct elevator opened. There were my things.

I got on and pushed the door hold button again. This time, I kept my foot in front of the door as I picked up the plastic bag and tried to maneuver myself so that I could put the plastic bag in the hall. This was not easy. I was really hurting by this time, and I could feel that my side had swelled up.

I got the plastic bag out and then tried the same maneuver to get the plant and my jacket. I was too weak by this time, lost my balance, and fell into the elevator. I hurt so badly and was so tired that, when the elevator opened on the lobby floor, I was still laying on the floor of the elevator.

There were a handful of student residents standing there looking at me. Now I had an elevator room full of "not quite almost doctors" all deciding that they would give me medical attention at once. I finally convinced them to just help me up off of the floor and explained what was going on.

They helped me to the second floor, picked up my things, and half carried me to the dorm room. They unlocked the door, put me into a bed in one of the bedrooms, and brought my things in. I had five of them in the dorm room with me. They got my pain pills out, gave me two of them, and told me to just lay still and sleep for awhile. One of the boys said he would check on me before he went on duty that night. I thanked them all, and, when they left, I burst into tears.

CHAPTER TWENTY-FIVE

✸

WHEN THE GOING GETS TOUGH, THE TOUGH KEEP GOING, AND GOING, AND GOING...

When I woke up the following morning, I no longer had to worry about a bowel movement. I had diarrhea. Now not only did my side hurt, but so did my ass. I decided I needed to wash up real good. I had been too tired and too sore, not to mention too weak, last night to even think about it.

My resident friend had returned as promised to made sure I was comfortable and had given me my pills before he went on duty. He left me a number to call him. I explained that the phone in the room only received calls and that I couldn't make calls from it. I would have to go down to the lobby to do that. He asked if he should check on me when he got off duty. I asked when that would be, and he said at six in the morning. I declined his offer and thanked him for his help. He said he would look in on me the next day.

After sitting on the leaky toilet (they hadn't fixed it yet) for most of the morning, I finally was able to wash myself. I wasn't allowed to take a shower, so I decided to just run some water in the tub, kneel, and wash off.

When I looked at my incision in the mirror, I had most of the residents on our floor banging on my door because of the blood-curdling scream I let out. Not only did I have an incision from my belly button to somewhere in the middle of my back, but I was also orange from the waist to the knees, and they had *stapled* me shut. I was picturing, in my mind, the doctor with a staple gun putting me back together.

I put my robe on and poked my head out the door to let the residents on the floor know that I was okay and that I wasn't being murdered. I told them I had just seen my incision for the first time. They nodded like they understood and drifted back into their rooms.

I rinsed off the orange paint the best I could and washed my hair. It really needed it. After that, I called the doctor's office.

On the phone I was greeted with, "Where are you? Why aren't you over here?"

I told them I was calling to make my appointment. I was informed that my appointment was fifteen minutes ago. Since I didn't know anything about that, I told them that I knew absolutely nothing about it. They told me to come on over. I asked if a car would be picking me up. I was told that there was no car and that I should just walk over. That meant another four-block-long walk. I got dressed and headed out.

It took me a while to get there, and I was pretty tired and weak. The doctor saw me and asked how I was doing. I said for him not to ask that question because I might really tell him. He said I should be able to go home in a week. I said that I planned on going home as soon as he removed the metal staples from my body so that I wouldn't set the alarms off at the airport.

He also thought Lois was still in town, and, when I told him I was alone at the dorm, he wasn't a happy camper. I stuck my tongue out at him. I told him that I had no intention of staying in that deathtrap of a hospital; it was a health hazard.

He told me to be sure to rest and not to walk around too much. I just looked at him like he had grown two heads. I told him that he had been the one to make me walk all the way from the dorm over to his office. He said he was sorry and that I should go back to the dorm and to bed. Nobody offered to give me a ride back.

I asked about a shuttle service. There was none. If you are over a mile from the building, they have a shuttle service. If I wanted to move back to the hotel, they had a shuttle service. Since I was only three-quarters of a mile away with my insides about to fall out, I didn't qualify for a ride. I was told to go back to the dorm and to bed and to rest. Don't walk around too much.

I left; if I had stayed, there would have been dead bodies all over his office. I then walked to the hospital to visit Betty; so much for taking their advice.

CHAPTER TWENTY-SIX

"NOW YOU'RE TRYING TO KILL MY SISTER!"

When I got to the hospital, I went immediately to get a diet coke from the vending machine. To this day I have to have pop, water, or iced tea by me at all times. When I got to Betty's room, it was to find her on the toilet in her bathroom, sweating profusely, and completely incoherent. The nurse in there with her was asking another nurse to "call the doctor, stat"!

I pushed them both away and started giving orders.

"Get me some juice with sugar, *now*!" I yelled.

They ran and did as I asked, and I got it down Betty.

"You fools over insulated her!" I shouted at them.

If you remember, my sister was a diabetic. They had been regulating her insulin since the transplant, and, because of all the different medications she was on, they had yet to get it right. Once I had her back in bed and back to normal, I was furious.

This hospital was the most incompetent place I had ever seen. Now they were trying to kill my sister. The sooner she was out of here, the better, was the way I was seeing it. I stayed with her for most of the day. I went down to the cafeteria to eat then headed back to the dorm to rest for a while and to take a pain pill.

I walked back to the hospital early in the evening to visit and left by seven-thirty so I wouldn't be on the streets after eight when the vampires started to roam. Considering how long it was taking me to walk the three blocks from the hospital to the dorm, I barely made it in time.

My resident was pacing the lobby when I came in. At least someone was concerned about me. He said I should be in bed resting, not walking all over Chicago. I agreed with him, but there wasn't anything I could do about it. My sister needed me, and, besides, it was the doctor himself who had started my exodus in the first place. He took me up to the dorm room made sure I took my pills, made sure I was comfortable, then left for his shift at the hospital for the damned.

Now I was back in the dorm with the two TV sets that got different channels in each room. That night, I would watch one TV and then move to the other room to watch the other TV since I could only get the two channels. Both TV sets started having reception problems. I was finally able to get one TV to work pretty well. Pretty well, that is, if I stood holding the rabbit ears in one hand with my other arm outstretched and resting one leg on the bed beside the TV. Since this was a bit uncomfortable, I gave up and decided to go to bed.

The next day I had to make the same hike two or three times during the day, and I needed my rest. So far, just in this one day, I figured I had walked about five miles. Not bad for my first day out of the hospital and for someone who is supposed to be recovering from major surgery.

CHAPTER TWENTY-SEVEN

✹

BETTY IS RELEASED FROM THE HOSPITAL FROM HELL

On Wednesday, Betty has convinced the doctors to let her out of the hospital and so she could move over to the dorm. She neglected to tell them that her son wouldn't be arriving until Thursday evening.

I got her all packed up with the help of all the nurses. We were loaded down with a suitcase and a *very big bag* of medication. She had tons of anti-rejection medication that she had to take, and she had to learn a strict schedule, which we had all written down for us. I would be alone trying to get the skunk pills down her throat.

They come up with a nice wheelchair for her and left me to carry the suitcase. Betty had the pills in her lap; a nurse carried the plants and stuffed animals that she had accumulated over her stay there. Notice, I had one potted plant after my whole side was ripped out, and she gets the royal treatment. I would be holding this kidney over her head for the rest of her life!

When we got downstairs, they loaded her into a van and started to shut the door. Apparently, she could ride to the dorm, but I couldn't. Now, I was still carrying a suitcase, and I was walking hunched over. Betty threw a fit. There is no other way to explain it. She refused to leave without me in the van. The driver argued that it was against policy; I thought she was going to slug him. He finally relented. We were driving over to the doctor's office, one block away.

We saw the doctor, and Betty was furious with the treatment I was getting. She let him have it with both barrels, and all of his staff too. When he was satisfied that she was calm, he examined her and then me. I could get my staples out tomorrow.

"Good, I'm flying home on Friday," I told him.

He argued and said that I should stay another week. I told him that my life was too short to remain in this hell hole another minute longer. He said that he would send my file to my doctor for a follow-up and told me to come in the morning to get the staples out.

I should explain here that, in trying to get my airline tickets, I was trying to get a medical discount. I didn't qualify for that. It didn't matter that I'd had major surgery or that I had donated a major organ. I had to be visiting a very sick relative. Betty was still in the hospital at the time I was calling for my reservations. Remember, I had to do this by using the pay phone in the basement of the dorm building. I finally got the discount ($600 difference) when the airline called the hospital and got the nurses to tell them my sister was a patient on the critical list. They lied for me; I figured they owed me at least that much.

I was scheduled to fly out on Friday afternoon from Midway Airport. I should also explain at this point that all of the major US airports were under strict security surveillance because of terrorist threats to bomb a US airplane. For me to try to get through security with my side stapled shut with metal was going to be very tricky.

When we left the doctor's office, they called the shuttle for Betty, and we again had to argue to get them to take me along. She still had a wheelchair; we swiped one from the medical building this time. At least, I swiped one. By this time, I was getting pretty good at it.

We finally made it back to the dorm. We had soup for dinner, and I had to force the pills down Betty's throat each time. It would take over a half an hour to get her medicine down her. We found that the boys had bought us some salami, crackers, and cheese, so we had a party watching TV that night.

The next morning, I had to walk back to the doctor's office to get my stitches out. I didn't like leaving Betty alone, but she said she would be fine. This time, luck was on our side, and nothing happened.

I was to have the staples removed, and they didn't want to do it. They said they would do it the next day. I left. Back at the dorm I packed; I was finally going home. It was going to be alright now. Betty and I had only one more day to go it alone. Boy, how wrong I was.

CHAPTER TWENTY-EIGHT
✤
WHEN IT RAINS, IT POURS

The next morning, Betty had to see the doctor again. She had to have blood work done every day to check her "crit" level, whatever that meant. I called for the shuttle. They said that we weren't far enough away for them to pick her up. I called the doctor's office to ask them to send the shuttle or someone to get her. No luck.

Now, it was October in Chicago. The week we were in the hospital had been sunny and in the 80s. This week, it was in the 50s and rainy. Betty had to be very careful not to catch a cold or to get sick. It was raining outside. I explained all of this to the personnel at the doctor's office. I was told to bring her over in the wheelchair.

I bundled Betty up in sweaters and a jacket and a blanket and gave her the umbrella to hold over her head. I was in my jacket and wind suit; I had no umbrella over me. I had to push her the three-quarters of a mile to the doctor's office. When we got there, I was soaked, and Betty was chilled. They took her blood and then decided to take a look at me.

"You're all wet!" says Tom.

"No kidding, Sherlock," I responded. "It's pouring out, in case you haven't noticed. We had to walk over here."

"You should have used an umbrella," he replied.

If I'd had the umbrella at that moment, I would have opened it up in a place where the sun never shines. I just glared at him. I told him that we had an umbrella and that Betty had used it. I, on the other hand, did not have one, and, even if I did, I couldn't have used it and pushed the wheelchair at the same time. He responded by telling me to make sure Betty didn't get cold or wet.

"I'll keep that in mind," I said. "Oh, by the way, what about me?"

I took the questionable look on his face to mean, "So? What about you?"

My stitch-removal was postponed until the following day. They told me I had been doing a little too much and wasn't healing quite as fast as they would like. Imagine that!

I bundled Betty back up, and we headed back to the dorm. Jeff, Betty's son, arrived that afternoon; I finished packing and was relieved that I would finally be going home the next day.

At least, I figured, I wouldn't have any more problems.

Oh, yeah? Guess again.

CHAPTER TWENTY-NINE

ON A WING AND A PRAYER

 The next morning, I again walked over to the doctor's office to have my staples removed. Betty had an appointment in the afternoon. Jeff was there and would drive her over in the afternoon.
 They still didn't want to take the staples out. I had to get through airport security, and wearing metal in my side wasn't going to cut it. They removed them and put some special tape on me to "hold me together."
 I left all excited. I was finally going home!
 Jeff took me to Midway Airport. At the check-in counter, the girl asked me some questions because I was flying under a reduced ticket for visiting a critically ill relative. I told her that my sister was in the hospital in critical condition because of kidney failure. She was sympathetic about it.
 "Yes," I said, "and, while I was visiting her, I gave her one of my kidneys."
 Then she looked up at me. I had her full attention now. She asked

why I needed the medical discount if that was the case. I told her that, no, I hadn't qualified for it, but visiting my sister did. Since we were in the same hospital, we visited frequently. I, too, had been on the critical list. She stamped my ticket, and I now had to make it through the security check.

Without the metal staples, the security check was fine. I still walked all stooped over, and people tended to stare at me.

I was finally on the plane. I looked out the window of the plane and could see the Chicago skyline and beautiful Lake Michigan. I pulled the shade down. I didn't want nightmares, and I was sleepy.

There was supposed to be a wheelchair waiting for me at the Minneapolis airport to take me to the flight to Eau Claire. I got off the plane. No wheelchair. I figured that this just couldn't be happening to me. I was close to home. This was a friendly part of the country; they certainly wouldn't forget about me. I waited, and I waited. I went to the check-in desk just as the check-in crew was getting ready to leave.

I explained to them, in as short a version I could (which wasn't easy), why I needed the wheelchair. My plane was to leave in less that half an hour. My flight was scheduled to leave from *the other side* of the Minneapolis airport. They didn't know anything about a wheelchair.

I started the long hike across the *very large* Minneapolis airport. People stared at me; I must have looked a sight. I was all hunched over and limping by this time. I had to stop to rest. The time that my flight was to leave was getting close. I had to go downstairs to catch my flight. It was difficult. I was exhausted, out of breath, and leaning on the stairwell.

Finally, a nice old man asked if he could help. I explained my situation, again in an abbreviated format. He immediately shouted at the top of his lungs for help. I had all kinds of help then. They finally got me in a wheelchair and a kind attendant checked me in. He never left my side until my flight left. I had to take a commuter plane that only holds eight people, so he had to wheel me out to the airplane. He helped me up the stairs and got me to my seat. The attendant on the plane said she would help me off when we landed.

We were finally off. These little planes are not fun. I swear, the pilot hit every bump and crevice in the runway before we finally took off. I was in agony. As soon as we were in the air, I promptly fell asleep. I awoke as soon as we landed because I felt it all over my body, especially on the side where my kidney had once been.

I was finally home. I got off the plane and was greeted by one of my friends from work who took me home.

I'm afraid the story doesn't end here. You see, I still had a husband at home who was recovering from a stroke. I never did get a chance to just rest and heal. But that is another book.

Did I ever tell you about my trip to Yugoslavia during the war?